THE DEVIL IN THE LAW

A Judicial Moral and Juridical Decline

J. MINOS SIMON

J. Minos Simon
P. O. Box 52116
Lafayette, Louisiana 70505

Library of Congress Card Catalog Number 99096804

Hardcover ISBN 0-9675053-0-5

Printed in the United States of America.

THE DEVIL IN THE LAW

A Judicial Moral and Juridical Decline

TABLE OF CONTENTS

ACKNOWLEDGMENT

I would be remiss in my sense of obligation were I not to acknowledge my debt of gratitude to my paralegal, Amanda Darby, for her tireless efforts in putting this book together in final form for the printer. She proofread the final transcript ... but before doing so, she labored tirelessly tracking down and verifying the legal citations of each case reviewed and discussed in this book. She made corrections, correlated footnotes to the text, and as that text was improved upon or changed, she did it all over again. And through it all she was faithful and loyal to the project, indulging the author's whims which intruded, however infrequently, and distracted from her efficiency. She made easy what appeared to me to be insurmountable. For that I am truly grateful.

DEDICATION

I dedicate this book to my wife, Jeanie Holmes.

PREVIOUS BOOK BY J. MINOS SIMON

LAW IN THE CAJUN NATION

(Simon was portrayed in the HBO movie "Judgment.")

CHAPTER ONE

THE AMERICAN MIRACLE

The date is March 4, 1789. The Continental Congress is in New York to commence proceedings to adopt a new Constitution. The night before, the guns of the battery had been fired to bid farewell to the old confederation. A general joy pervaded the whole city in tune with the important and memorable event. Excitement was in the air. It was cold and there was a scarcity of fuel to fight the cold but this day was special. All hardship was overlooked. Parties were everywhere and houses were open to guests. Boards were piled with venison, bear, wild turkey, fish and other meats in abundance. There was as well an abundance of ale, strong beer, cider and punch. This was a time for celebration. There was widespread hope that this day would truly begin the United States of America. The new Constitution, proposed by southern states and worked out in Philadelphia barely a year earlier, was innovative, providing a two-house Legislature, a Chief Executive, and a Supreme Court. It promised a new era for all people, not only in America but in the world. Such was the feeling of the day. That feeling was fueled by the soaring words harnessed by Jefferson in verbalizing the Declaration of Independence more than a decade before. It was an anticipated birth long acoming arousing the passions and anticipatory excitement akin to those who stand in wait of a newborn babe.

The euphoria notwithstanding, this moment had its share of frustration. The weather and road conditions took their toll. A number of Representatives timely arrived, among whom were Fisher Ames and Elridge Jerry of Massachusetts, John Gilman of New Hampshire, Samuel Huntington of Connecticut. And a number of senators, too: Robert Morris and William Maclay of Pennsylvania, and William Few of Georgia. But a quorum was not present. Vice President John Adams timely arrived but the proceedings could not start until a quorum was present. George Washington, elected President by acclamation, was at Mount Vernon, some four to five days away, awaiting his call. Days of waiting went by. March 31st came and went. The mood of euphoria soon changed into a mood of gloom, with its attendant spin-off of irritation and exacerbation. Eventually on April 6, 1789, Richard Henry Lee of Virginia arrived — the same Richard Henry Lee, who as delegate to the Continental Congress on June 7, 1776, made the original motion that the colonies were "free and independent states", the synoptic prototype of Jefferson's Declaration of Independence. Now a quorum is present in both houses. Congress is convened. Washington is certified, and the government of the "United States of America" begins a month and two days late.

Much had preceded this historic event. During the more than ten year interval, there was the Declaration of Independence, the Revolutionary War and the creation of the Continental Congress, all infused with political intrigues, rebellion against the Crown, conflicts between the industrial development of the north and agrarian culture of the south and the nagging slavery problem. Enough to stupify even the most stout-hearted men. Where to begin? What to do? History recorded many revolutions but none ever resulted in the creation of a government whose powers originated with the people. The word democracy had been used many times over to identify a variety of organized governments, including aristocratic and oligarchic types, but never as a government of the people, for the people and by the people as proclaimed by Abraham Lincoln in his Gettysburg Address. Slavery, reaching back into antiquity, including whites, blacks, Jews and people of all stripes, had never been extirpated by any form of government, until the adoption of our Constitution crafted by the founders of our nation, made this possible.

So looking across the horizon of history, our founding fathers could find little comfort and less encouragement to make their vision of human freedom a reality for mankind. Even a visit to ancient wisdom was equivocal and non-reassuring, that the ideals of human freedom, which flamed within the souls of our founding fathers, could ever be more than a quixotic notion — a practically unreachable goal.

They could consult Aristotle (384-322 B.C.), as surely they did, and come away from that visit more than a little disheartened. It was Aristotle's view, as expressed in his **Politics**, that at best, democracy was only "tolerable" and seemed capable of degenerating into despotism and tyranny. Plato, who was sixty-one when Aristotle entered the Academy at Athens, thought even less of democracy than did Aristotle. In Plato's view, as expressed in his **Statesman**, he found democracy "in every respect weak and unable to do either any great good or any great evil".

And in the **Republic**, he places democracy at only one removed from tyranny, saying tyranny "arise naturally out of democracy, and the most aggravated form of tyranny and slavery out of the most extreme form of liberty".

But this pall of gloom hanging over the prospect of democracy was not to lead the ancient Greeks into emulating the barbarians of their time. There was, in Greek culture, a reverence for human dignity and, therefore, a natural inclination, at least among the intellectual elite, to self-discipline and moral and intellectual integrity, so classically exemplified by the act of Socrates choosing death to the compromise of his intellectual integrity. It was a human quality whose vision reached beyond the mundane tumult and preoccupations of trade and commerce, of conquest and power. It was a quality that would inspire them to dethrone extant monarchies and strive to replace them with a more dispersed sovereign of feudal aristocracy, evolving inexorably into an expansion of the circle of power that would include other members of society. There are many great figures involved in this histolic and diastolic historical, political process, and many significant epochal events rich in courage, physical bravery, betrayals, brutality, patriotism and victories and defeat. The purpose here is not either to recount or examine all of them, but only to say that all attempts at instituting a real democracy failed for the lack of universal suffrage. An example of these attempts, however, served to inform the founders of America of the pitfalls to avoid and of the intricate and delicate nature of their democratic enterprise.

The Solonian Revolution, 594 B.C., a warless and non-violent event, appears to be a good beginning point. Draco's code, which preceded this revolution, did nothing to relieve the oppressive financial burdens of the non-aristocratic class or to mitigate the exploitation of the weak by the strong. It was a code of law heavily weighted in favor of the aristocratic rich. As the seventh century (B.C.) drew to a close the bitterness of the helpless poor against the rich brought Athens to the edge of revolution. The poor, who witnessed their situation worsen with each year, with the army in the hands of their masters and the corrupt courts deciding every issue against them, could think of no alternative to revolution to bring about some semblance of fairness and to effect a thoroughgoing redistribution of wealth. Because of the poverty of the working person and farmers, the rich were unable to collect debts legally due to them and invoke ancient laws that were cruelly oppressive of their debtors. And they prepared to defend themselves by force against the threatening mob. It is at this point of high societal tension that Solon prominently appeared on the stage of history.

Before his call to official duty Solon had taken to trade and became a successful merchant with far-flung interests that gave him wide experience and travel and acquired an exceptional reputation for integrity. In 594 B.C., a representative of the middle class asked Solon, then in his mid 40's, to accept election nominally as archon but with dictatorial powers to soothe the rumbling social war. He accepted. His first measures were simple but constituted drastic economic reforms. He made no move to redivide the land, which disappointed the extreme radicals and the debt burdened poor, but on the other hand, however, as Aristotle said, he canceled "all existing debts, whether owing to private persons or to the state" and in one fell swoop purged attica lands of all mortgages. Furthermore, all persons enslaved or attached for debt were released; those sold into servitude abroad were reclaimed and freed and such enslavement was forbidden for the future.

He made a stab at establishing democracy, an effort considered dramatic for his time. Solon divided the free population of Attica into four groups according to their wealth: first, were the 500 bushel men whose annual income reached 500 measures of product; second, those whose income was between 300 and 500 measures; third, those with income between 200 and 300 measures; and fourth, all other free men. This formula excluded a large segment of the population, such as serfs, tenants, tillers, and other laborers not earning the necessary measures contained in the formula. The first class was eligible to archonship or to military commands; the second class was eligible to lower offices and to the cavalry; the third was privileged to join the heavy-armed infantry; the fourth was expected to provide the common soldiers of the state. This unique classification established a new principle of "timocracy", a government by honor or prestige as determined by taxable wealth. The old senate was open now to all members of the first class but still with supreme authority over the conduct of the people and the officers of the state. He then created a council of 400 to which each of the four tribes elected a hundred members. Those on this council selected, censored and prepared all business that could be brought before the assembly.

Beneath this oligarchic superstructure, Solon placed fundamentally democratic institutions. He revived the assembly of Homer's day and all citizens were invited to join in his deliberations. This assembly annually elected from among the first 500 bushel men and the archons and they could at anytime impeach or punish these archons regarding their official conduct. Also he granted to the lowest class of citizens the full parity with the highest class in being eligible to select by lot to a body of 6,000 jurors that formed the various courts before which all matters except murder and treason were tried and to which appeal could be made from any action of the magistrates.[1]

Though Solon reached out to the poor to give them some power in government, the real and controlling power remained in the hands of the rich. They were the first to scoff at the power of the poor in their capacity as court jurors. They laughed at the Constitution, saying that the wise would plead and the fools would decide. However faulted his Constitution may have been, his work marked the end of government of numerous and almost daily changeable decrees and the beginning of government by written and permanent law. When asked what made an orderly and well constituted state he replied: "When the people obey the rulers and the rulers obey the laws." Here was a statement made more than two thousand five hundred years ago, which captures one of the essential components of the ideal of modern day democracy. And as we shall see later in the discussion regarding decisions of our Supreme Court, there is a raging debate that some of the Justices of the Supreme Court, in rendering their decisions, are themselves not obeying the laws as intended by our founding fathers. One can picture Solon looking down on this intellectual tumult with an inscrutable Mona Lisa smile on his face.

At the age of sixty-six, after serving twenty-two years, he retired into private life and set out to observe the civilizations of Egypt and the East. When he returned to Athens to die he saw in his last years the overthrow of his Constitution, and the establishment of a dictatorship in 546 B.C. And with that dictatorship his dream of enlarging the circle of power to include some of those other than the rich and powerful came to an end.

The downfall of Greece began circa 160 B.C. when the Romans started their conquest in earnest. Greek civilization died in A.D. 325 when Constantine founded Constantinople. The legacy of that civilization lived on as the infrastructure for future generations and future nations. The democratic idea of a government responsible to the governed, of trial by jury, and of civil liberties of thought, speech, writing, assemblage and worship have been profoundly stimulated by Greek history [among other things such as Olympic games, the conception of self-containment and of self-control, the cult of health and natural living]. Even Christian theology and practice stem in large part from the mystery religions of Greece and Egypt.[2] As Henry James Maine, English jurist and historian (1822-1888) said, “Except the blind forces of nature, nothing moves in this world which is not Greek in its origin”.

The founders of America were aware of the history, which preceded the creation of America. They were aware of the Roman conquest; of the confrontation of Christ and Caesar, which brought about the disintegration of the Roman empire; of the Dark Ages; of the Renaissance; of the Reformation, and of the Enlightenment which pitted the age of reason against the orthodoxy and dominion of religion. This rebellion against the crown was headed by the intellectuals of France, among whom notably were Voltaire, La Mettrie, Diderot, d’Alembert, Grimm, Helvetius and d’Holbach. The collective thrust of these intellectuals was recorded in a publication known as the Encyclopedie. On the political front the Catholic Church was the immediate target, because it was the power behind the state. It was a powerful organization owning a large share of the national wealth and soil. It held thousands of peasants in practical serfdom on its lands. It controlled nearly all the schools and universities and in fact Voltaire was tutored by Jesuits. It denounced as heresy any teaching contrary to its own, and used the state to enforce its censorship over speech and press. This intellectual tumult was a precursor to the French Revolution. It put on display the tyranny and oppression of a state sponsored religion. The founders of our nation learned a valuable lesson regarding the practical effect of an interlocking relationship between church and state. That lesson is reflected by the content of the First Amendment to the United States Constitution where it was postulated:

> "Congress shall make no law respecting an establishment of religion, or prohibiting the free exercise thereof . . . "

Our forefathers thus made sure that the violence, bloodshed, and chaos which characterized the French Revolution, and which catapulted Napoleon to the absolute power of emperor, never would find residency within the continental United States of America.

American colonies were under the yoke of British colonialism and the colonists were not free to engage in commerce or trade in an unfettered manner as they may have wished for their survival and success. They were burdened with elementary rules and regulations as almost to pauperize the enterprising Americans. England required that certain commodities produced in America could be sold only to English merchants, at prices dictated by England and transported only on English vessels. Exorbitant taxation further crippled the economic growth of the colonies, frustrated the colonial entrepreneurs, and, not only alienated the colonists but created a deep seated antipathy against the crown. The more England intensified its dominion over the colonies, the more the colonists' resentment grew, stirring about in the vortex of rebellion and culminating in war.

A succinct statement of the seeds of revolution is captured by an astute commentator: [3]

> "Not unreasonably, Britain decided that the cost of defending and administering the vast North American Em-

pire should be shared by the colonies. For Parliament was convinced that they benefitted most from the imperial ties, which was not as it was meant to be. Indeed, an investigation by the Lords of the Treasury into why the Molasses Act of 1733 had failed to raise the anticipated revenue had concluded, on October 4, 1763:

> We observe with concern that through neglect, connivance, and fraud, not only the revenue is impaired, but the commerce of the colonies is diverted from its natural course and the salutary provisions of many wise laws to secure it to the mother country are in great measure defeated.

The colonies, their lordships concluded, were swindling the mother country! Parliament's response: the American Revenue Act of 1764, known as the Sugar Act, which put duties on molasses, sugar, wine, silk, and linen and required the colonies to buy rum from Great Britain. (Rum, John Adams would write, "was an essential ingredient in American independence.") The Sugar Act was the work of one Charles Jenkinson, whose intent went far beyond raising revenue.

> The increase in our Colonies is certainly what we wish, but they must increase in a manner as will keep them useful to the

> Mother Country. . . With this view all the provisions of [the act] are formed, and as far as it is necessary for this purpose to restrain the commerce of our Colonies, it is an evil to which I think they ought to submit for the good of the whole.

> The Sugar Act was followed by the Currency Act, denying the colonies the right to issue paper money, and the Stamp Act of 1765, requiring stamps on all newspapers, pamphlets, legal papers, bills of lading, mortgages, skins, parchments, college diplomas, almanacs, calendars, playing cards, tavern licenses, and advertisements. Lawyers, printers, editors, merchants and clergymen were hardest hit . . .

> Parliament had misjudged the mood in the colonies; the Stamp Act caused an uproar. "Taxation without representation is tyranny!" went the cry through Colonial taverns and towns."

Rapprochement with England was no longer feasible. Reconciliation was impossible. The colonies had a choice: submit or triumph. And they opted to triumph. But revolution alone was not enough to sustain the creation of a new and independent nation. There had to be a belief, an idea, an ideal. To mimic the construct of other nations would rob the Founders of their innovative skills, of their creativity and of their sense of human destiny. They felt in their hearts that fate had appointed them to construct an article of governance and faith - a governance whose power must originate with the people, and a faith which recognizes the existence of a Creator and that man was created in His image. It was a powerful moment in human history. They could scan the landscape of history and find no precedent. At best, history taught them what not to do. Many philosophers, poets and scholars had spoken to human dignity, but none had ever constructed a system of governance whose primordial component was rooted in the universal concept of human dignity.

It was not enough to protest. There had to be a clean break from England. There was a need to take a political step that would effect an amalgam of purpose and destiny for all citizens of the colonies. And, it was agreed that this first step was a declaration of independence from England. From that moment forward it would be them against us. Thomas Jefferson was selected to draft the Declaration of Independence. He agreed to do so and he did so. No one else could have done a better job but he drew upon the lessons of history, upon his sense of humanity, and upon the voice of the Universe and reduced these into one simple but powerful statement:

> "We hold these truths to be self-evident; that all men are created equal; that they are endowed by their Creator with certain unalienable rights; that among these are life, liberty and the pursuit of happiness. That, to secure these rights, governments are instituted among men, deriving their just power from the consent of the governed; that, whenever any form of government becomes destructive of these ends, it is the right of the people to alter or abolish it, and to institute a new government, laying its foun-

> dations on such principles, and organizing its powers in such form, as to them shall seem most likely to effect their safety and happiness."

This declaration is a mix of God and country. It is a declaration that people have unalienable rights prior to government. Among these rights are freedom of thought, freedom of will, freedom of speech, freedom of privacy, freedom of religion, freedom of association, and freedom of conscience. But the exercise of such freedom is not a reckless one. It has a built in moral constraint. For example, one is free to cry fire in a crowded theater. But a moral imperative of responsibility prohibits one from *falsely* crying fire in a crowded theater. These unalienable rights are mightier than the sword, as demonstrated by the struggle of the early Christians, by Mahatma Ghandi of India and Martin Luther King, Jr. of America.

"To secure these rights", Jefferson declared, "governments are instituted among men, deriving their just powers from the consent of the governed". That declaration was the birth announcement of a new social and political philosophy, the affirmation that power resided in the people. For two hundred years these words would shake the world order. People of all classes, all religions, and all colors in the two centuries since would strive for that promise. Once uttered, the words could not be destroyed; once heard, the words could not be forgotten. It was not until 1789 that the Ten Amendments to the Constitution were introduced in the House of Representatives for eventual adoption. The first Ten Amendments were intended to apply against the federal government and federal officials. It was only after the adoption of the Fourteenth Amendment that the original Ten Amendments were made applicable against the states and their officials.

The creative activity of this social and political revolution found deep roots in the Williamsburg intellectual community. Washington, Henry, Wythe, the Randolphs, the Lees, Jefferson, Madison, Marshal, Monroe, to mention only the most illuminaries, all came together in some grand cosmic accident. Meeting and stimulating one another in a village, which had only three diversions: talk, scholarship, and politics. These diversions centered about the villages' three main enterprises, the university, the capitol, and the taverns. The dye was now cast. The moment had arrived, when this social and political philosophy was to be tested in the crucible of reality.

CHAPTER TWO

U. S. SUPREME COURT

THE EARLY DAYS

Article III, Section 1 of the United States Constitution provides for the creation of a Supreme Court. In part pertinent, Section 1, declares that:

> "The judicial power of the United States, shall be vested in one Supreme Court, and in such inferior courts as the Condress may from time to time ordain and establish."

Section 2 extended its judicial power to all cases, in law and equity, arising under the Constitution or laws of the United States and treaties among other powers.

Many were the skeptics who did not believe that this branch of government was equal in power to the executive and legislative branches.

The view was that the Court could decide cases but it had no enforcement power. It had no police or army under its jurisdictional command. These critics downgraded the Supreme Court to but a notch above a sinecure. To the chagrin of the skeptics the test of the Court's power was soon to come, and it would come packaged in a Pandora's box of absolutism being the ultimate arbiter of controversial issues involving the executive and legislative branches of the federal government, and after the adoption of the Fourteenth Amendment, that power would extend over controversial issues involving every state of the union.

Early political thought regarding the perceived nature of the new nation was extremely controversial. Political parties, reflecting the dominant political differences, were formally organized. There arose consequently, the Hamiltonian Federalist and the Jeffersonian Democrats-Republicans whose members were fiercely anti-Federalist. The Federalists represented a loose interpretation of the Constitution; northern states and northern interests; and big business, big gevernment, big banking and big industry. The Democrats (Republicans) were essentially southern farmers, small businessmen, and artisans demanding a strict interpretation of the Constitution, state's rights, and a small central government. Hamilton saw the nation as a great industrial power and designed his Treasury programs accordingly. Jefferson envisioned an agrarian democracy such as he had known and seen working well in Virginia. The division of political thought between Hamilton and Jefferson went much deeper. Hamilton was pro-British and Jefferson was pro-French. While Jefferson was for a strict construction of the Constitution, he was not for that reason indifferent to the minority of the political process. In his Inaugural Address, he called upon all citizens to remember the "sacred principle, that though the will of the majority is in all cases to prevail, that will, to be rightful, must be reasonable; that the minority possess their equal rights, which equal laws must protect, and to violate which would be oppression. Having banished religious intolerance, we have yet gained little if we countenance a political intolerance, as despotic as wicked and capable of as bitter and bloody persecutions."[4] Jefferson's vision of the strength of this nation depended not upon enlargement of power for the national government, but upon the people and their loyalty to self government. He dismissed Hamiltonian strong central government view in these words "sometimes it is said, that man cannot be trusted with the government of himself. Can he then be trusted to govern others? Or have we found angels in the form of kings to govern him?"

Never had there come into existence a written Constitution whose power originates with the people, whose governmental structure consisted of three distinct and independent branches, the executive, legislative and judicial, the so called check and balance system. Inevitably their separateness and their power vis a vis each other would become tested.

In 1803, while France churned in the wake of its revolution, and one year before Napoleon was crowned emperor, a tug of war erupted in America. It was a war between the executive and judicial branches of government. James Madison, Secretary of State of the United States, refused to deliver the several commissions of appointed Justices of the Peace in the District of Columbia. These justices had been appointed by President Adams with the advice and consent of the Senate. The commissions in question were in due form, signed by President Adams and the seal of the United States was duly affixed to the commission. But Secretary Madison refused to deliver these commissions to the appointed justices. Legal action was presented to the Supreme Court to compel

Madison to deliver to those justices their commissions. Madison defended by interposing executive privilege based on the separation of power among the executive, legislative and judicial branches of government. The Court rejected this defense. In so doing the Court pointed out that the delivery of the commissions by Secretary Madison was but a ministerial duty as to which he had no discretion. The appointment was complete except for delivery of the commission. The Supreme Court then concluded that Secretary of State Madison was subject to being directed to deliver the commissions to the applicants. In the course of its opinion, the Court held that the Constitution represented the fundamental and paramount law of the nation; that it is the duty of the Supreme Court to assess the constitutional validity of any statute or official act; and that decisions of the Supreme Court become the paramount law of the nation. ***Marbury v. Madison*** [5]. Thus it was that this supposedly toothless tiger showed its fangs. It was the beginning of an evolving judicial drama, which variably, from time to time, would exemplify judicial rectitude, judicial activism, and judicial misadventure.

The Fifth Amendment to the United States Constitution in part pertinent stated that "No person shall . . . be deprived of life, liberty or property, without due process of law; nor shall private property be taken for public use, without just compensation."

It was the Democrats (Republicans) who insisted that a Bill of Rights must be included as part of the Constitution. The Federalists responded that the Constitution itself was a sufficient guaranty against government infringement of individual rights. They further argued that a Bill of Rights was not necessary because all rights not granted to the federal government were reserved by the people. The Jeffersonian Democrats used the absence of a Bill of Rights as an argument against the adoption of the

Constitution. Their argument was persuasive and very effective and was eroding public support for the adoption of the Constitution. The Federalists relented and adopted ten amendments to the United States Constitution, including the Fifth Amendment just mentioned. The reach of these amendments, particularly the Fifth Amendment, was soon to be tested.

In 1833, the City of Baltimore, in the exercise of its corporate authority over the harbor, the paving of streets, etc., engaged in construction activities which altered the natural course of certain streams of water which flowed from the range of hills bordering this city. The streams artificially altered, carried down with them the hills and the soil over which they ran, large masses of sand and earth which the streams deposited along and widely in front of plaintiff's wharf. The consequence of that artificially induced change in the natural water flow rendered the water near plaintiff's wharf so shallow that it ceased to be useful for vessels of any important traffic. Plaintiff claimed that these changes were brought about without his consent, that the changes rendered his wharf business nonexistent for commerce, and that he had suffered great damage of income and property. He sued the City of Baltimore for his damages. Essentially he claimed that the city had confiscated his property without due process of law and had effectively taken his property without just compensation, in violation of the Fifth Amendment to the United States Constitution.

The issues as just composed were presented to the United States Supreme Court. Chief Justice Marshall wrote the opinion of the court. At the outset he postulated that "The question thus presented is, we think, of great importance, but not of much difficulty." In rationalizing the Court's decision, he pointed out that the Constitution "was ordained and established by the people of the United States for themselves, for their own government, and not for the government of the individual States." He further observed that the States had reserved unto themselves all powers of government not granted to the Federal government. Each state, therefore, had the power to provide protection to its citizens against any state infringement of their rights. He furthermore insisted that it was error to insist that the Constitution "was intended to secure the people of the several States against the undue exercise of power by their respective state governments." Finally Justice Marshall concluded that neither the due process clause nor the prohibition against the taking of property without just compensation residing in the Constitution applied to the States. He therefore dismissed plaintiff's claim (***Barron v. Baltimore***) [6]

As harsh as the decision of the United States Supreme Court may appear on the face of this litigation, the result reached by the Court should not have been unexpected. The founders knew that the power of the federal government consisted of that power delegated to it by the States. It was because the delegates were jealous of the power of their states and fearful of the power of the federal government that they adopted the Tenth Amendment, which reads:

> "The powers not delegated to the United States by the Constitution, nor prohibited by it to the States, are reserved to the States respectively, or to the people."

This decision in fact mirrored Jefferson's vision of the relationship between the national government and state governments. He insisted on the strict interpretation of the Constitution, State's rights, and a small central government. Underlying such a philosophy was his claim that the relation of the individual to the nation was not direct, but was to be mediated by the citizen's participation in local political entities, such as municipalities. Tocqueville describes such a link between liberty and democracy in these words:

> "Town meetings are to liberty what primary schools are to science; they bring it within the people's reach, they teach men how to use and how to enjoy it. A nation may establish a free government, but without municipal institutions, it cannot have the spirit of liberty." [7]

Such a notion proclaims that the States, in exercising their residuum of sovereign power, each in its own way and in its own time, would enact those laws perceived by each to be suitable to protect and promote the welfare of its citizens. History teaches, however, that the states did not measure up to the demands of fundamental equality and due process. The rule of men polluted the unalienable rights of citizens. Slavery existed as a scourge of liberty. It seared the souls of those whose conscience viewed such human degradation as repugnant to the human spirit. This lack of redress, of rescue from the Supreme Court regarding the abuse of citizens by the states, as exemplified by the Barron case, was to continue for at least another thirty-five years, until the adoption of the Fourteenth Amendment in 1868.

CHAPTER THREE

THE FOURTEENTH AMENDMENT

In 1853, Dred Scott took center stage in the evolving drama of the judicial branch of government. [8] Dred Scott was a slave residing in St. Louis, Missouri, and a citizen of Missouri. He married Harriet Scott, a slave. Of that marriage two girls were born, Eliza and Lizzie Scott. Scott filed a lawsuit in the United States Court for the District of Missouri and in his complaint he affirmatively stated that John F. A. Sandford was a citizen of New York, and that he, Scott, his wife and children were citizens of Missouri. Federal courts, then and now, have jurisdiction to resolve any controversy between citizens of different states. Scott invoked that jurisdiction. And his substantive complaint was that Sandford was abusing him, his wife and his two minor daughters and holding them as slaves. Sandford defended Scott's claim by affirmatively stating that Scott was not a citizen of the State of Missouri, sufficient to sustain a citizenship of the United States, "because he is a Negro of African descent, his ancestors were of pure African blood and were brought into this country and sold as Negro slaves, therefore, federal courts were without jurisdiction to adjudicate Scott's complaint of enslavement."

Chief Justice Taney wrote the opinion of the Supreme Court. He stated the question before it as follows:

> "The question is simply this: Can a Negro whose ancestors were imported into this country and sold as slaves, become a member of the political community formed and brought into existence by the Constitution of the United States, and as such become entitled to all the rights and privileges and immunities guaranteed by that instrument to the citizen? One of these rights is the privilege of suing in a court of the United States in the cases specified in the Constitution."

Since the nature and extent of the jurisdiction of the federal judiciary constituted the pivotal issue to be determined, Justice Taney first addressed the outer contour of that issue. In doing so, he reminded that the jurisdiction of the court was specified as "enumerated in the Constitution" and "neither the legislative, executive nor judicial departments of the government can lawfully exercise any authority beyond the limits marked out by the Constitution." He considered the issue before the court to be "a very serious question" and further observed that such a question was being presented "for the first time." He stated further that the only matter presented was whether or not slaves "are citizens of a state, in the sense in which the word 'citizen' is used in the Constitution of the United States." He acknowledged the power of the states to enact their own laws under the reserve powers of the Tenth Amendment. He further concluded that it was not within the province of the Supreme Court to decide "upon the justice or injustice, the policy or impolicy" involved. Honoring the separation of power expressed in the Constitution, Chief Justice Taney stated that any decision as to the justice or injustice or the policy or impolicy of laws "belonged to the political or law-making power; to those who formed the sovereignty and framed the Constitution". In differentiating the duty of the court vis-a-vis the "law-making power" of our nation, Justice Taney stated that the court is to interpret the constitution "with the best lights we can obtain on the subject, and to administer it as we find it, according to its true intent and meaning when it was adopted." That statement represents classic Jeffersonian Doctrine: strict construction of the Constitution and laws in keeping with the "true intent and meaning" of the Constitution "when it was adopted". As the subsequent decisions of the Supreme Court demonstrate, there has arisen a raging dispute among members of our juridical society regarding the applicability of the original intent of the Constitution as the indispensable tool to determine the reach and scope of our federal constitution.

The Court then proceeded to assess the civil status of Dred Scott and members of his family. In doing so the Court stated that for more than a century before the Negro was considered a being of "inferior order" and so far inferior that they had no rights which the "white men was bound to respect". As a consequence the Negro "might justly and lawfully be reduced to slavery for his benefit. He was bought and sold, and treated as an ordinary article of merchandise and traffic, whenever a profit could be made by it." Taney further stated that such treatment "was regarded as an axiom in moral as well as in politics." He then stated that it was necessary to refer to such historical facts in order to determine whether the constitution, conferring rights on citizens, "was intended to include" Negroes. In deciding that the constitution did not intend to include Negroes, Justice Taney referred to provisions in the very constitution to support his conclusions. As he was to say, there were two clauses in the constitution which pointed "directly and specifically to the Negro race as a separate class of persons" not included as "citizens of the government then formed". One of these clauses said the Court "reserves to each of the thirteen states the right to import slaves until the year 1808, if it thinks proper". The other provision in the constitution engaged the states, pledging themselves to each other "to maintain the right of property of the master, by delivering up to him any slave who may have escaped from his service". As barbaric as such a political notion might appear, Taney observed that the men who "framed" the Constitution were "high in literary acquirements" and "high in their sense of honor, and incapable of asserting principles inconsistent with those on which they were acting". Furthermore he observed that such men "perfectly understood the meaning of the language they used, and how it would be understood by others". The court then concluded that, honoring the intention of the framers of the constitution, the conclusion was inescapable that the constitution was not intended to "embrace the Negro race" as citizens of the United States. The court further observed that citizenship in a state did not constitute citizenship of the United States. In other words, even if Dred Scott was a citizen of Missouri, that citizenship status did not make him a citizen of the United States. In so concluding Chief Justice Taney postulated:

> "And no law of a State, therefore, passed since the Constitution was adopted, can give any right of citizenship

outside of its own territory."

The court then rendered judgment dismissing Dred Scott's lawsuit on the basis that, since Dred Scott was not a citizen of the United States, he was not a citizen within the jurisdiction of the federal judiciary and therefore, without capacity to invoke the jurisdiction of the federal courts.

As barbaric as the result of that decision is, attributing to these judges the elementary human impulse of compassion for those less fortunate, it took uncommon courage for the justices to render that decision. They had to reject the demands of the heart for rescue. The justices were moved by the demands of the rule of law. They were moved by respect for the integrity of the constitutional structure of our system of government. In other words, the power conferred on the court gave rise to the duty of its judges to interpret the Constitution "with the best lights we can obtain on the subject, and to administer it as we find it, according to its true intent and meaning when it was adopted". No matter how barbaric the result of any decision might be, the court has no jurisdiction to change the law, which brings about a barbaric result. The removal of any evil or offensive notion existing in a law enacted by the national congress or legislatures of the states must be done by the legislative branch of government by the enactment of new laws which eliminate that offensive law as interpreted by the courts.

The Dred Scott decision, because it cut so deeply into the concept of human dignity, emphasizes more poignantly than otherwise possible, the concept of ordered liberty, and the need to hold the three branches of government accountable to the people in such a manner as will maintain the structure and functional characteristic of our institutions of freedom. When one branch of government intrudes upon the other, there occurs to some extent, a meltdown of the structural integrity of government, and a corresponding diminution of our concept of ordered liberty.

This 1857 decision of the Supreme Court told the black citizens of America and citizens of the world that the yoke of slavery was to remain as an anomalous part of the liberty fabric of our nation. This decision stirred the pot of controversy in America over slavery. And also spawned hopelessness and desperation among the black community, and to some significant extent, pangs of conscience among the white community. This desperation incited John Brown to rebellion, choosing death over slavery. It engaged Lincoln and Douglas, then presidential candidates, to serious debate over slavery. Lincoln was later to say that the big test was how long a nation can endure half free and half slave.

The Civil War did what the national congress refused or failed to do. During the reconstruction era following the Civil War the national congress proposed and the states ratified three amendments to the Constitution, the Thirteenth, Fourteenth and Fifteenth Amendments. The Thirteenth Amendment, ratified December 6, 1865, prohibited slavery in the United States. The Fifteenth Amendment ratified February 3, 1870, guaranteed to citizens the right to vote, regardless of "race, color or previous condition of servitude". The Fourteenth Amendment ratified July 9, 1868, brought about a fundamental change in the legal relationship between the states and the national government as to the rights of citizens in every state of the Union. In part pertinent, the Fourteenth Amendment provides:

> "All persons born or naturalized in the United States, and subject to the jurisdiction thereof, are citizens of the United States and of the state wherein they reside. No state shall make or enforce any law which shall abridge the privi-

> leges or immunities of citizens of the United States; nor shall any state deprive any person of life, liberty or property, without due process of law; nor deny to any person within its jurisdiction the equal protection of the laws."

Thus in one fell swoop, the judicial branch of the nation was empowered to adjudicate the constitutional liberties of every citizen offended by any state or any state official. Such an amendment was revolutionary especially when viewed in the context of the decision by the Supreme Court to the effect that the equal protection and due process clause of the Fifth Amendment did not apply against states and their officials, leaving the states with power to enact laws regulating the rights of its citizens that were impervious to any judicial scrutiny by the Supreme Court. The judicial power conferred upon the federal courts was not only unprecedented, but was awesome in dimension and content. Federal judges were now empowered to declare and define the "unalienable" rights of every citizen of the nation. This power conferred is made egregiously awesome because federal judges are appointed for life and are accountable to no one (except impeachment), in some instances, not even God. The potential of that unconditional power for good or evil as to citizens' "unalienable" rights is demonstrated by notable decisions rendered after the adoption of the Fourteenth Amendment.

The judicial drama beginning in the ***Marbury v. Madison*** case would be revitalized and shaped by the judicial branch of government in ways that would not only defy the intent of our founders in the creation of our national constitution, but also in ways that found anchorage in the personality and the social and political proclivities of federal judges, to the dismay and discontent of the American people.

In 1873 the Fourteenth Amendment received judicial scrutiny from the Supreme Court for the first time. ***Slaughterhouse Case.***[9] At that time there were in excess of thirty animal slaughterhouses in the New Orleans area. For the most part these slaughterhouses were located along the Mississippi River because water transport was the major transport system for such animals.

On March 8, 1869, a Louisiana statute entitled an act to protect the health of the City New Orleans and to locate the stock landings and slaughterhouses and to incorporate a corporation known as the Crescent City Livestock Landing and Slaughterhouse Company was enacted. This corporation was granted the exclusive power to operate a stock landing and slaughterhouse to slaughter all the animals and declared that after June, 1869 it would be unlawful for any other person to establish any other stock landing or slaughterhouses within the City of New Orleans including the parishes of Orleans, Jefferson and St. Bernard or to slaughter any animals in that geographical area at any place other than the slaughterhouses established by the corporation. And after the effective date of the act, all stock landings and slaughterhouses within the area contemplated by the state law were to be closed and it was no longer lawful for anyone to slaughter cattle, hogs, calves, sheep or goats, the meat of which was destined for sale within the parishes mentioned. The act further provided that the company would receive for every animal slaughtered in its buildings, certain prescribed fees "besides the head, feet, gore, and entrails of all animals, except of swine". The monopoly of the newly formed corporation was for a period of twenty-five years.

The Slaughterhouse Association and members of that association as well as other involved persons filed a lawsuit in the state District Court claiming that this state statute deprived them of their property without due process and deprived them of equal protection, granting a monopoly of the slaughtering business to this newly created corporation. The State Supreme Court denied relief. On appeal, the Supreme Court, in a 5 - 4 decision, denied their claims and dismissed their lawsuit, and thus affirmed the decision of the state Supreme Court.

The slaughterhouse owners, who were soon to be excluded by the operation of the state statute, argued to the Supreme Court that this state statute denied to them their "privileges and immunities" which included the right to engage in a gainful occupation, in violation of the Fourteenth Amendment. They argued that the Fourteenth Amendment was adopted for the specific purpose of giving protection to the citizens of the various states regarding their "privileges and immunities", especially in view of the earlier decisions of the Supreme Court to the effect that the "privileges and immunities" contained in the Fifth Amendment could not be applied against the states, even if the "privileges and immunities" of citizens were denied by state action. In its analytical search for a reason to support the court's decision, the majority conceded that the "privileges and immunities" clause of the Fifth Amendment was indeed broad, and not yet fully defined; it was stated that the privileges and immunities clause "embraces nearly every civil right for the establishment and protection of which organized government is instituted". And while government protected its citizens against the deprivation or impairment of these rights, the enjoyment and exercise of those rights were subject to "such restraints as the government may prescribe for the general ***good of the whole***".

The more the majority scrutinized the numerosity of rights included within the generic term "privileges and immunities", the more incredible it appeared to their minds that the Fourteenth Amendment was ever intended to confer upon the Supreme Court such awesome power over the states. The majority underscored their judicial doubt stating that, if true, the Supreme Court would be established as:

> " . . . a perpetual censor upon all legislations of the states, on the civil rights of their own citizens, with authority to nullify such as it did not approve as consistent with those rights, as they existed at the time of the adoption of this amendment. The argument, we admit, is not always the most conclusive which is drawn from the consequences urged against the adoption of a particular construction of an instrument. But when, as in the case before us, these consequences are so serious, so far-reaching and pervading, so great a departure from the structure and spirit of our institutions; when the effect is to fetter and degrade the state governments by subjecting them to the control of Congress, in the exercise of powers heretofore universally conceded to them of the most ordinary and fundamental character; when in fact it radically changes the whole theory of the relations of the state and federal government to each other and of both these governments to the people; the argument has a force that is irresistible, in the absence of language which expresses such a purpose too clearly to admit of doubt.
>
> We are convinced that no such results were intended by the Congress which proposed these amendments, nor by the Legislatures of the state which ratified them."

The court then rejected the application of the Fourteenth Amendment as a basis to determine the rights of the slaughterhouse owners. The majority then concluded that what was at issue were the privileges and immunities "which belonged to citizens of the states as such". And on that account "they are left to the state governments for security and protection".

The court then turned its attention to the nature of the state legislation and concluded that the state of Louisiana was simply exercising its police power to protect the health of the consumers. Justice Miller further declared:

> "The power here exercised by the Legislature of Louisiana is, in its essential nature, one which has been, up to the present period in the constitutional history of this country, always conceded to belong to the states, however it may now be questioned in some of its details."

To infuse by osmosis into the Fourteenth Amendment the privileges and immunities of the Fifth Amendment the court said, would be "to transfer the security and protection of all the civil rights which we have mentioned, from the states to the federal government". That the majority refused to do.

While Justice Field, dissenting, agreed that the Louisiana statute did not violate the rights of the slaughterhouse owners, he, accompanied by three other justices, disagreed with the majority as to the applicability of the Fourteenth Amendment. On this issue Justice Field said:

> "The question presented is therefore, one of the gravest importance not merely to the parties here, but to the whole country. It is nothing less than the question whether the

> recent amendments to the federal constitution protect the citizens of the United States against the deprivation of their common rights by state legislation. In my judgment, the Fourteenth Amendment does afford such protection and was so intended by the Congress which framed and the states which adopted it."

The purpose of the adoption of the Fourteenth Amendment, said Justice Field, was:

> "to place the common rights of American citizens under the protection of the national government."

Justice Field further stated that the Fourteenth Amendment did not create any new rights, it merely absorbed existing rights of the citizens of our nation and prohibited state governments from denying these rights to its citizens. This conclusion is reflected in his affirmative statement:

> "The Amendment does not attempt to confer any new privileges or immunities upon citizens or to enumerate or define those already existing. It assumes that there are such privileges and immunities which belong of right to the citizens as such and ordains that they shall not be abridged by state legislation."

The rights contemplated by the Fourteenth Amendment were identified by Justice Field in these words:

> "That amendment was intended to give practical effect to the declaration of 1776 of unalienable rights, **rights which are the gift of the Creator; which the law does not con-**

> **fer but only recognizes**."

Justice Swayne, another dissenting justice, chastised the majority for having exceeded the parameter of authority of the Supreme Court by an interpretation that engaged the majority in the making of a law not intended. The following comments are exceedingly noteworthy as they relate to the duty of the Supreme Court and to the integrity of the separation of powers of our nation. Said Justice Swayne:

> "This court has no authority to interpolate a limitation that is neither expressed nor implied. Our duty is to execute the law, not to make it . . . It is necessary to enable the government of the nation to secure to everyone within its jurisdiction the rights and privileges enumerated, which, according to the plainest considerations of reason and justice and the fundamental principle of social compact, all are entitled to enjoy."

Finally, summarizing his assessment of the judicial apostasy of the majority, Justice Swayne metaphorically declared:

> "To the extent of that limitation it turns, as it were, what was meant for *bread* into a *stone*."

Though distracted by the fundamental differences of the justices as to the reach of the Fourteenth Amendment, the decision is an object lesson in the tension between the interest of the states on the one hand, as opposed to the rights of the citizen on the other hand.

Drawing a bright line between these two contending claims, that is in harmony with the philosophical thrust of our national charter, has always proven to be difficult, though not insurmountable. With the passing of time this difficulty has gotten progressively worse. This worse condition is not due to any progressive complexity of legal issues, nor to the factual matrix of the legal issues presented. This worse condition is due to the methodology utilized by the Supreme Court in evaluating the substantive value to society of the moral, religious and liberty issues in controversy. The slaughterhouse court adopted a very simple but philosophically consistent interpretative approach, in harmony with the national charter. It applied the paradigm that validates any legislation that may impinge upon, in whole or in part, the individual's right under the constitution. That paradigm contemplates a critical analysis of such legislation to determine if it "secures the general comfort, health and prosperity of the state". In reaching such a conclusion it then gives effect to the constitutional calculus that "all kinds of restraints and burdens" must be endured by the citizens "in order to secure the general comfort, health and prosperity of the state". The majority opinion further amplified on this paradigm of judicial interpretation by stating that "the good of the whole" supercedes the liberty rights of an individual where these contending claims are in collision. The decision of the ***Slaughterhouse case*** acknowledged that the legislation was reasonable and served a governmental purpose for the good of the whole, i.e. the societal good. In that respect that decision exemplified the "spirit of liberty" emphasized by Jefferson in his inaugural address, where he called upon all citizens to remember the "sacred principle, that though the will of the majority is in all cases to prevail, that will, to be rightful, must be reasonable; that the minority possess those equal rights, which equal laws must protect, and to violate which would be oppression".

This balancing of the interest of the state (majority will) and the rights of the minority has been the preoccupation of the Supreme Court since the inception of our national charter. And over the years since the slaqghterhouse case the guiding calculus of that balancing act has undergone a metamorphic change, a change which disconnects the individual from his government, disregards his concept of morality, and denigrates his right to meaningful protests. Vis a vis his government and the policy of his government, the American citizen, by and large, is but a flotsam adrift in the tumultuous sea of judicial misadventure. Subsequent decisions of the Supreme Court hereafter discussed will demonstrate this conclusion.

CHAPTER FOUR

INDIVIDUAL RIGHTS TRUMP MAJORITY RULE

1897-1937

The latter part of the nineteenth century witnessed the growth and expansion of the industrial might of America. This growth was accompanied and aided by excessive tariffs or excessive duties exacted on the import of goods. The political muscle of the industrial empire was as vast as the industrial output. And as a concomitant part of that growth was the industrial exploitation of labor, male and female.

During the 1888-1889 campaign for the presidency, the primary issue was one of tariff. The Republican Party chose General Benjamin Harrison of Indiana, a grandson of "Tippecanoe" as their candidate. The Democrats chose Grover Cleveland. During the campaign the Republicans accused Cleveland of advocating "free trade", a cry made familiar during the 1996-97 debate over NAFTA (North American Free Trade Agreement). Harrison received 233 electoral votes to Cleveland's 168, and thus, Harrison was elected President, though Cleveland received a plurality of some 100,000 of the popular vote over that of Harrison.

America then was not as we know her today. In the cities there were "no subways, few electric cars, and for the most part buses and horse-cars jogged along at about four miles an hour". Further, there were no automobiles and for the most part everyone "relied upon a horse and carriage, if he had any conveyance of his own". Soaring above the condition of the ordinary citizen were the great titans of the new business era, men of the type of the elder J. P. Morgan, of James J. Hill, William H. Vandenberg, Carnegie, Frick, William H. Clark and Rockefeller. "They were men of wide economic but intensely narrow social vision, and of colossal driving power and iron wills. They could lay their economic plans with imperial vision in time and space, but for the effect of their acts on society they cared nothing whatever." This historian further asserted that "they claim the right to rule the economic destinies of the people in any way that would inure to their own personal advantage". [10] It apparently was this controlling power which led the court to unwittingly aid the industrial barons in their effort to exploit the industrial laborers. The following notable decisions exemplify this unholy alliance.

In 1897 the Supreme Court effected the final interment of the slaughterhouse case regarding the applicability of the Fourteenth Amendment against the states. The slaughterhouse court held that the Fourteenth Amendment did not reach the states because otherwise the court would then become "a perpetual censor upon all legislations of the states, on the civil rights of their own citizens, with authority to nullify such as it did not approve as consistent with those rights, as they existed at the time of the adoption of this amendment". The slaughterhouse court then concluded that "no such results were intended by the Congress which proposed these amendments, nor by the legislatures of the state which ratified them". But the 1897 Supreme Court stated emphatically that indeed that which was considered unintended by the slaughterhouse court was in fact the intention of the Fourteenth Amendment; that the Supreme Court was conferred the power to be a "perpetual censor upon all legislations of the state, on the civil rights of their own citizens" with authority to nullify any such state law that deprives state citizens of their "unalienable" rights. ***Allgeyer v. State of Louisiana.*** [11] As in the ***Slaughterhouse case***, the ***Allgeyer*** case rose out of Louisiana. It involved a state statute which prohibited any persons or corporations from dealing with maritime insurance companies "that have not complied with" Louisiana law. The insurance company involved in that case was charged with violating the statute, issuing a policy of marine insurance without complying with the state law that required such an insurer to have an agent in the state of Louisiana, and otherwise complying with the state laws regulating those engaged in the insurance business in Louisiana. The defendants conceded that the insurance company was domiciled in the state of New York; that the contract of insurance was confected in the state of New York, and that it had not complied with Louisiana law just mentioned. The defendants, however, asserted that the Louisiana law deprived them of the right of contract secured to them by the Fourteenth Amendment. In the course of the opinion, the court held that the defendant would be subject to the penalties mentioned, unless

> "it violates one of those unalienable rights relating to persons and property that are inherent, although not expressed, in the organic law."

The court concluded that Louisiana was attempting to give effect to their laws beyond the boundary of the state of Louisiana and was therefore, unconstitutional because it violated the rights of the defendant under the Fourteenth Amendment. In assessing the reach of the "unalienable" rights of the Declaration of Independence, and contemplated by the Fourteenth Amendment, the court enumerated these rights as follows:

> "The 'liberty' mentioned in that amendment means, not only the right of the citizen to be free from the mere physical restraint of his person, as by incarceration, but the term is deemed to embrace the right of the citizen to be free in the enjoyment of all his faculties; to be free to use them in all lawful ways; to live and work where he wills; to earn his livelihood by any lawful calling; to pursue any livelihood or avocation; and for that purpose to enter into all contracts which may be proper, necessary, and essential to his carrying out to a successful conclusion the purposes above mentioned."

The court buttressed its conclusion by adopting the dissent of Justice Bradley in the ***Slaughterhouse case***:

> "The right to follow any of the common occupations of life is an unalienable right. It was formulated as such under the phrase 'pursuit of happiness' in the Declaration of Independence, which commenced with the fundamental proposition that 'all men are created equal; that they are endowed by their Creator with certain unalienable rights; that among these are life, liberty and the pursuit of

> happiness'. This right is a large ingredient in the civil liberty of the citizen".

Significantly, this court is reminding America that the "unalienable rights" of every citizen are those which are "endowed by their Creator", and not by government but existing prior to government.

This thought, this notion, this philosophy of government resides at the very core of our liberty concept. It is made up of the aggregation of countless human values—religious, moral and ethical values. And these represent the rudder of our destiny as a people. But later decisions of the court demonstrate an egregious departure from these human values. In the process of this departure the court has adopted an interpretative approach which excludes any consideration or assessment of these values. The right of abortion is an example of this approach. If, as the court says, our Creator endowed each with "unalienable rights", then we must say as to the right of abortion, that our Creator endowed a female with the power of procreation and the anatomy to nurture that procreated being to its birth. But the court has stated that a female has the "unalienable" right to control her body, which includes the right to abort the life of that procreated human being. In other words, her Creator "endowed" her with the power of procreation, and during her pregnancy her Creator "endowed" her with the "unalienable" right to kill the procreated being, without cause, but based entirely on her wish or whim. If that be so, then our Creator must be the most egregious monster ever conceived by man. This brief diversion is an aid to give the reader an anticipatory view of the wrong headed action of the court in future cases regarding the "unalienable" rights of the American citizen.

The court in ***Allgeyer*** did not hold that the right of the insurer trumped the majority will of the people in the enactment of the legislation involved. It simply held that the contract in controversy was completed outside of the state of Louisiana and therefore, the statute could not be given extraterritorial effect, and therefore, was unconstitutional. The court declared that it did not intend to hold that in no case can the state exercise its police power, that is, the collective right of citizens which prevail over the individual rights of citizens. The significant statement of the court as to that principle is verbalized in these words:

> "The foregoing extract (other cited cases) have been made for the purpose of showing what general definitions have been given in regard to the meaning of the word 'liberty' as used in the amendment, but **we do not intend to hold that in no such case can the state exercise its police power**. When and how far such power may be legitimately exercised with regard to the subject must be left for determination to each case as it arises."

Thus as of 1897, the expansive "unalienable rights" of the individual were subject to the right of the majority to enact legislation for the protection of the safety and welfare of the whole, provided it is reasonable.

1905 instances high drama in the evolution of the judicial department of our nation. It involved a cataclysmic collision between the majority rule of our democracy versus the "unalienable" rights of the individual. It engaged the court in second guessing the ends to be accomplished by the state law at issue. More than this, it involved the court in substituting its own judgment for that of the state legislature regarding the need of such a law. Though wearing the mask of sophistry, the court traveled into the domain of judicial heresy by making law rather than executing the law, an adventure expressly prohibited by the court's earlier decision in the slaughterhouse case. That judicial proscription was verbalized by Justice Swayne when he stated that "our duty is to execute the law, not to make it".

The decision under discussion occurred in the case of ***Lochner v. New York.***[12] In that case, exercising the power reserved under the Tenth Amendment, the people of New York, acting through their legislature, enacted a law which prohibited bakery workers from working more than ten hours per day or in the aggregate, sixty hours per week. A bakery employer was found guilty of violating that state law. In his appeal to the appellate courts of New York, the employer contended that the bakery law violated his "unalienable" right of contract, thus existed in violation of the Fourteenth Amendment. The highest court of the state of New York rejected the employer's constitutional attack because the court concluded that the law in question was one regulating the public health of its citizens in that the evidence presented to the state court indicated the conclusion that the occupation of a baker or confectioner was unhealthy and tended to result in diseases of the respiratory organs. On appeal to the Supreme Court a majority of five to four reversed the state court decision on the grounds that the state law violated the employer's "unalienable" right of freedom of contract. The majority stated that the issue before it was,

> " . . . a question of which of two powers or right should prevail, — the power of the state to legislate or the right of the individual to liberty of person and freedom of contract."

Because this decision instances the first judicial effort of a movement away from Jefferson's majority rule and toward the individual's "unalienable" rights, in the process of striking a balance between these conflicting claims, a somewhat penetrating analysis of this decision will be helpful. It will be helpful to understand the nature of the seminal seed planted by the decision, and the ease with which the fruits of that seed gave rise to the dominion of the individual's rights over the majority will of society.

Justice Peckham, speaking for the majority, acknowledged the rule of law as exemplified by earlier cases of the Supreme Court, that the right of individuals must yield to the police power of the state in safeguarding the safety and health of its people. In his analysis of the state law involved, he acknowledged that a bakery employee "does not appear to be as healthy as some other trades". But that was not a sufficient basis to deny the constitutional right of an individual to freedom of contract. Contrary to the standard of judicial review on such a question, Justice Peckham insisted that before a state could interfere with the individual's constitutional right to freedom of contract, it must first be concluded that there existed a "material danger to the public health or to the health of the employees", if the hours of labor involved in this state law "are not curtailed". Finding the existence of no "material danger" the majority held that the state law violated the employer's constitutional right to freedom of contract.

The dissent was vigorous. Justice Holmes dissenting, observed the case was decided upon an "economic theory". But he affirmed that an analysis of the validity of such a theory was not for the court to decide because, as he said, "I strongly believe that my agreement or disagreement has nothing to do with the right of a majority to embody their opinions in law". Further Justice Holmes observed that the jurisprudence of the Supreme Court acknowledged that "state constitutions and state laws may regulate life in many ways which we as legislators might think as injudicious, or if you like as tyrannical, as this, and which, equally with this, interfere with the liberty to contract." Further, he observed that the Constitution was not intended to "embody a particular economic theory". The Constitution "is made for people of fundamentally differing views". And the accident of the court finding certain opinions "natural and familiar, or novel and even shocking, must not conclude the court's judgment on the question whether statutes embodying them conflict with the Constitution of the United States". Finally Justice Holmes stated:

> " . . . I think that the word 'liberty', in the 14th Amendment, **is perverted** when it is held to prevent the natural outcome of a dominant opinion, unless it can be said that a rational and fair man necessarily would admit that the statute proposed would infringe fundamental principles as they have been understood by the traditions of our people and our law."

Justice Harlan, joined by Justice White and Justice Day, dissenting, disagreed with the standard of review of the majority opinion. He grounded his opinion on previous decisions of the Supreme Court pointing out that the case law was to the effect that regulations regarding trade, businesses and occupations, "are questions for the state to determine, and their determination comes within the proper exercise of the police power by the state". Such regulations are not to be rejected, unless the regulations are so utterly unreasonable and extravagant in their nature and purpose, as to unnecessarily and in a manner "wholly arbitrary" interfere with or destroy the rights of citizens. The dissent further observed that the constitutional liberty of every person does not constitute "an absolute right in each person to be at times and in all circumstances wholly freed from restraint". Further Justice Harlan postulated:

> " . . . There are manifold restraints to which every person is necessarily subject for the common good."

Further the dissent stated that if there be doubt as to the validity of a statute:

> "That doubt must therefore be resolved in favor of its validity, and the courts must **keep their hands off**, leaving the legislature to meet the responsibility for unwise legislation."

Justice Harlan observed that studies concerning the hazards which the bakery industry generated showed that "the constant inhaling of flour dust causes inflammation of the lungs and of the bronchial tubes, . . . the long hours of toil to which all bakers are subjected produce rheumatism, cramps and swollen legs". The dissent further concluded that the New York statute constituted a legitimate exercise of the police power of the state, constituting an hierarchy of command which must prevail over the constitutional liberties of the individual, thus echoing Jefferson's inaugural statement that when "reasonable" the "sacred principle", that "the will of the majority" in "all cases is to prevail".

POST MORTEM. The New York legislation presented to the court an economic theory, "laissez faire", (anything goes) which unrestrained was harmful to laborers; that the long hours of labor enhanced the potential of that harm; that placing restrictions on the number of hours per day, per week a laborer could be compelled to work would reduce the potential harm and thus protect and promote the health of the laborers, so said the people of New York.

But the Supreme Court majority disagreed. The disagreement, however, related not to the **existence** of the potential harm, but to the **degree** of harm relied upon by the people of New York for the enactment of the law in controversy. Speaking for the majority Justice Peckham insisted that there must be a showing that there existed a "material danger to the public health or to the health of the employees" before the right of contract of a citizen could be disregarded. In increasing the degree of proof from potential harm to actual "danger", the majority thereupon held that this state law violated the right of contract of the employer and employees.

Four of the nine justices of the court disagreed with the majority ruling. The dissenting justices found ample evidence of the harm against which the state sought to protect the laborers involved. Further Justice Holmes observed that previous rulings of the Supreme Court acknowledged that "state constitutions and state laws may regulate life in many ways" even in ways that judges "might think as injudicious, or if you like as tyrannical, as this, and which, equally with this, interfere with the liberty to contract".

The fundamental disagreement among judges at the highest level of government indelibly establishes that minimally there existed a doubt about the legal quality of the New York State law in controversy. But the majority refused to apply the existing rule of law which, as stated by dissenting Justice Harlan:

> "That doubt must therefore be resolved in favor of its validity, and the courts must **keep their hands off**, leaving

> the legislature to meet the responsibility for unwise legislation."

Through the art of semanticism the court majority substituted its view of the element of harm in controversy for that of the people of New York and thereby created a different law. Such an act excites to memory a recollection of Justice Swayne's judicial "crie de couer":

> "This court has **no authority** to **interpolate a limitation** that is neither expressed nor implied. Our duty is to **execute the law, not to make it** . . .. "

By 1890 farmers and laborers were at the mercy of the economic titans. The Vanderbilts controlled the major railroads. The farmers could not secure reasonable transport rates while big shippers like Rockefeller drove his own freight-rate bargains with the rail magnates. The poor entertained the belief that there was "a great conspiracy on the part of the very rich to ruin the poor". Buttressing this view was the knowledge that Vanderbilt enlarged his private fortune from about 10 million dollars to more than 100 million dollars. The industrial titans were insouciant to the struggles of the working man. When public interest was suggested to the younger Vanderbilt, who was associated with his father, he uttered his famous answer, "the public be damned". The labor unions attempted to negotiate equitable wages and conditions for the laborer. Capital met this request with the importation of strikebreakers. H. C. Frick, Chairman of the Carnegie Brothers and Company, hated the working man. In 1892 when the union contract expired, rather than negotiate in good faith, the owners delivered an ultimatum to the union to accept what was offered and if the union refused to accept the offer, the owners would no longer deal with the union, but only with the men as individuals. The laborers went on strike. The strike spread to other commercial enterprises which finally resulted in the great railroad strike at Chicago. Soon the union learned that even its strongest organization was powerless before organized capital. Violence erupted between striking laborers and the strikebreakers in many areas of the country.[13] In 1898, in the midst of this economic turmoil and social unrest, the National Congress enacted a law designated as "an act concerning carriers engaged in interstate commerce and their employees". Among other things this act provided for arbitration of labor disputes and provided a penalty for an "employer who shall require any employee or any person seeking employment, as a condition of such employment, to enter into an agreement either written or verbal, not to become or remain a member of any labor corporation, association or organization; or shall threaten any employee with loss of employment" because of membership in such a labor union. This Congressional Act became the subject of constitutional attack, ***Adair v. United States***. [14]

In that case Adair, as an agent of the employer, Louisville and Nashville Railroad Company, fired one O. B. Coppage because of his membership in the Order of Locomotive Fireman, a labor organization. Adair attacked the constitutionality of the law in question contending that it violated the employer's freedom of contract.

The U. S. Senate Committee, speaking to the purpose or need of the legislation, in reporting to the whole senate, said:

> "The necessity for the bill arises from the calamitous results in the way of ill considered strikes arising from the tyranny of capital or unjust demands of labor organizations, whereby the business of the country is brought to a

> standstill and thousands of employees, with their helpless wives and children, are confronted with starvation."

The House committee on labor reported that:

> "Persons engaged in interstate commerce have been anxious to secure the enactment into law of such measure as would operate justly and effectively to put an end to the industrial wars that have resulted from disputes growing out of the questions of wages, hours of labor, and the conditions of employment between the employer and the employee."

In the lower court Adair argued that this congressional act deprived him of his unalienable right of freedom of contract in violation of the due process clause of the Fifth Amendment. The court rejected that contention after concluding that the congressional act reflected the legitimate exercise of the police power of Congress to protect the health and well being of employees engaged in interstate commerce activities. On appeal to the Supreme Court, that court reversed the lower court holding that that law violated the due process rights of the employer and employee to exercise their freedom of contract privilege.

In rationalizing its decision the court held that:

> "It was the right of the defendant (employer) to prescribe the terms upon which the services of Coppage would be accepted and it was the right of Coppage to become or not, as he chose, an employee of the railroad company upon the terms offered to him."

In other words the court postulated that the right to purchase or to sell labor was part of the liberty protected by the Fifth Amendment. Further said the court:

> "In all such particulars the employer and the employee have equality of right, and any legislation that disturbs that equality is an arbitrary interference with the liberty of contract which no government can legally justify in a free land."

Thus what was not so innocently done in the 1905 ***Lochner v. New York*** case now went full circle. As declared by the Senate Committee, managing the law in controversy through the congressional process, the purpose of the legislation was to protect "thousands of employees, with their helpless wives and children" who were "confronted with starvation". Moreover, the law was needful to avoid bringing the national business to a "standstill". One can think of nothing more pervasively imperative to justify the rights of the people to such legislation. But the Adair court ignored the need of the people for economic stability. It simply concluded that any legislation that "disturbs the employer and employees" freedom of contract constituted "an arbitrary interference" with their "liberty of contract which no government can legally justify in a free land". In so ruling the court hoisted the individual right of contract to the highest level of priority, towering over the right of the people to enact laws for the protection and welfare of the health of the people. In so doing, the court trampled underfoot the paradigm that validates any legislation that may impinge upon, in whole or in part, the individual's right under the Constitution. It should be recalled that this paradigm contemplates a critical analysis of any legislation to determine if it "secures the general comfort, health and prosperity of the state". This in turn gives effect to the constitutional calculus that "all kinds of restraints and burdens" must be endured by the citizens "in order to secure the general comfort, health and prosperity of the state". Thus it was that the court apotheosized the right of the individual and postulated it as the god to be worshiped by the people, while simultaneously denying the right of the people to embody their view or opinion in laws that reflected the majority view of what was good for the whole of America.

In 1901 the shot that killed President McKinley propelled Theodore Roosevelt into the presidency. The political bosses and big business interests had thought they had buried Roosevelt as presiding officer of the senate. McKinley's assassination would change all this. The age of electricity had arrived. In 1900 there were about 2,500 power stations, increasing rapidly each year. This electrical power brought about the marketing of enumerable sorts of electrical appliances, such as irons, dishwashers, etc. and the electric lights. Skyscraper buildings were mushrooming and by 1902, there was the Woolworth's Building in New York, 785 feet high. In 1895 there were but four motor cars registered in the whole country. By 1900 there were 8,000. There was a growing interest in communal rather than personal life. The reduction of costs in printing as well as the discovery of great profits in advertising brought about a formidable increase of circulation of low priced magazines such as Collier's, Munsey's, McClure's, the Cosmopolitan and others, including the Saturday Evening Post. As one historian stated, the "great change in the scale of business, the vast opportunities for sudden and incalculably great riches from stock watering and market operations, had gone to the heads of these leaders who were corrupting and threatening the whole of American life, growing colossally rich while wages were being lowered."[15]

Roosevelt, who was neither pro-labor nor pro-industry, reflecting on the attitude of the rich, wrote that "in their hearts they take the ground that to take legal proceedings against them when they violate the law and to endeavor to have them pay their proper share of the taxes is as much of an outrage as to excite the mob to plunder the rich". The leading writers of the period, including Jack London, Mrs. Wharton and John Fox, wrote articles dealing with the evils and scandals of the extant economic and political regime exposed also in such books as ***The Octopus***, ***The Pit*** and ***The History of the Standard Oil Company***. The economic oppression and the corruption of the time established deep discontent and mistrust of the people with their leaders. Many of the states enacted legislation to protect the people against the exploitation of labor by the economic giants of that era. Kansas was one of those states.

In 1902 the people of Kansas, acting through their legislature, enacted a law similar to the law involved in the ***Adair*** case, which made it unlawful for any individual or member of any firm or employee of any company "to coerce, require, demand or influence any person or persons to enter into any agreement, either written or verbal, not to join or become or remain a member of any labor organization or association as a condition of such person or person securing employment or continuing an existing employment" or continuing in such employment. The constitutionality of that statute was first challenged in the Supreme Court of the State of Kansas and eventually in 1915 in the United Sates Supreme Court, ***Coppage v. Kansas***.[16]

One Hedges was employed as a switchman by the St. Louis and San Francisco Railroad Company and was a member of the Switchman's Union of North America. Coppage, employed by the railroad company as superintendent, requested Hedges to sign an agreement to the effect that he would withdraw from the Switchman's Union while in the service of the Frisco Company. On presenting such an agreement, Coppage told Hedges that if he did not sign this agreement "he would not remain in the employ of the company". Hedges refused and was promptly fired. Coppage was charged with violating the state law against such agreements. The highest court of the state maintained the constitutionality of the statute. However, the Supreme Court reversed after holding the state law in question unconstitutional.

The rationale of the Supreme Court mirrored the Supreme Court's rationale in the ***Adair*** case: the statute violated the individual's freedom of contract. Justice Holmes again dissented, in essence stating that a workman "may believe that only by belonging to a union can he secure a contract that shall be fair to him". And such a belief could be held by a reasonable man to be proper, therefore, it can be enforced by law "in order to establish the equality of position between the parties in which liberty of contract begins".

Justice Day, dissenting, protested that the right of contract is "not absolute and unyielding, but is subject to limitation and restraint in the interest of the public health, safety and welfare". Justice Day further observed that the "legislature is, in the first instance, the judge of what is necessary for the public welfare".

This red tide of judicial indifference to the right of the people to provide for the health and welfare of society would continue spreading over the land for an additional twenty years. Even an attempt by the legislative body to fix minimum wages for women and minor children in the work place was rejected by the Supreme Court as existing in violation of freedom of contract, ***Atkins v. Children's Hospital***. [17] One of the female employees involved was employed as an elevator operator at a salary of "$35.00 per month and two meals a day".

This red tide was to experience an unexpected and fatal encounter with the Supreme Court in 1937.

Franklin Roosevelt, in 1936, fresh from his election as President, was committed to doing something about the decisions of the Supreme Court from 1897 to 1937 establishing a doctrine of law that made the right of the individual absolute and superior to the people's right to create laws to protect the health and welfare of American society. The Supreme Court's intransigence in holding its course for 40 years did not escape his attention. Shortly after his election it was reported that he would "pack" the court. There were then nine justices of the Supreme Court, (as now) and rumors resonated at the highest level of government that he would increase the number to 15. The 6 new members, joining hands with those who had dissented from the various opinions on this issue, would constitute a majority. There was then pending before the Supreme Court, the case of ***West Coast Hotel Company v. Parrish***.[18] It appears that the rumor of "packing" the court somehow translated into creating a new legal vision among the majority of the judges of the court regarding the triumph of individual rights over the good and welfare of the people.

The ***Parrish*** case was decided by the Supreme Court in 1937, argued in 1936. That case involved the constitutionality of a law enacted by the people of the State of Washington, acting through their legislature, which provided for minimum wages for women and the fixing of minimum wages for women and minors. That law was to all intents and purposes essentially the same law involved in the ***Atkins*** case where the court had declared such a law unconstitutional because it violated the right of individuals to freedom of contract. But this 1937 court expressly reversed the ***Atkins*** decision and all other similar decisions rendered for the 40 previous years. When addressing the "freedom of contract" concept this 1937 court said:

> "What is this freedom? The Constitution does not speak of freedom of contract. It speaks of liberty and prohibits the deprivation of liberty without due process of law. In prohibiting that deprivation, the Constitution does ***not*** recognize an ***absolute*** and ***uncontrollable*** liberty."

The court further postulated that the "liberty" safeguarded by the Constitution is "liberty in a **social organization** which requires the protection of law against the evils which menace the health, safety, moral and welfare of the people". The court echoed the paradigm controlling the court's approach to the validity of any law. And as earlier stated, that paradigm contemplates a critical analysis of such legislation to determine if it "secures the general comfort, health and prosperity of the state". And the corollary rule of law which provides that the citizen must endure "all kinds of restraints and burdens . . . in order to secure the general comfort, health and prosperity of the state". In echoing that fundamental principle of our democracy the court said:

> "There is no absolute freedom to do as one wills or to contract as one chooses."

And so it was that 40 years of judicial activism was interred. There was a dramatic return to the judicial philosophy of interpreting the Constitution "with the best light we can obtain on the subject, and to administer it as we find it, according to **its true intent and meaning when it was adopted**", as the court declared in the Dred Scott case. In that process the court gave effect to the paradigm of judicial interpretation that contemplates a critical analysis of legislation to determine if it "secures the general comfort, health and prosperity of the state". And on reaching such a conclusion that it does, this gives effect to the constitutional calculus that "all kinds of restraints and burdens" must be endured by the citizens "in order to secure the general comfort, health and prosperity of the state". Jefferson was back in the saddle. The devil in the law, which advocated and sustained the dominion of the right of the individual over that of the people, now was nothing but a moribund legal body, awaiting an unceremonial burial. But as we shall see by later decisions this devil which makes the individual's rights superior to the people's right to have their views embodied in law, would rise from the dead to wreak havoc once again on the right of the people to embody into law their moral and political views of what is good for America.

CHAPTER FIVE

FLAG SALUTING VS. FLAG BURNING

The most momentous event, exemplifying the national significance of our flag, occurred on the island of Iwo Jima in the South Pacific during the latter part of World War II. This event engaged several of our fighting soldiers, in combat with the Japanese soldiers for the conquest of Iwo Jima, to pause long enough to proudly plant our flag on an improvised pole. These were the same soldiers who dedicated their lives to the defense of America and in the process narrowly escaped being killed; these are the soldiers who witnessed the deaths of their comrades; who prayed for divine guidance and courage; and who steadfastly faced the perils of war yet to come. They knew the meaning of our flag. They were baptized in fire and death. They understood the human worth of our liberty concept, of our national devotion to the existence of God. They knew that these fundamental virtues of America were embodied in that flag. The planting of this flag was these soldiers' way to tell the world, and reassure America, that our flag was still there, as the inspiration to face death in the defense of America. The planting of that flag was an immutable attestation to the bravery and loyalty of those soldiers who forfeited their lives in the defense of our liberty. Symbols are generally accepted as the poetry of speech. The planting of that flag was the most profound poetic proclamation possible of the underlying and nurturing ideals of America. It lifted the spirit of every American who loves our ideals. This event is now memorialized by a monument at our nation's Capitol whereby the photograph of this event was cut in stone to last forever.

History credits Betsy Ross with the creation of the American Flag. Reliable history tells that in May of 1776, George Washington, then the head of the Continental Army, Robert Morris, an owner of vast amounts of land, and perhaps the wealthiest citizen in the colonies, and Colonel George Ross, a respected Philadelphian and also the uncle of her late husband, John Ross, appeared at her home and asked her to put together the first American Flag. She finished with the flag in early June of 1776 and in July the Declaration of Independence was read aloud for the first time at Independence Hall. Amid the celebration the liberty bell tolled, heralding the birth of a new nation, and the flag unfurled as the poetic expression of American ideals. The contagion of this poetic speech spread quickly and has been sustained by the human spirit ever since. Witness the following poem: [19]

"A nation thrills, a nation bleeds,
A nation follows where it leads,
And every man is proud to yield
His life upon a crimson field

For Betsy's battle flag."

And another poem: [20]

"'Twas red with the blood of freemen
and white with the fear of the foe;
And the stars that fit in their courses
'gainst tyrants its symbols know."

Lucy Larcom in *"The Flag"*, stirs the human spirit in her poetic statement: [21]

"Each red stripe has blazoned forth
Gospels writ in blood;
Every star has sung the birth
Of some deathless good."

In 1940 the Supreme Court was called upon to legally assess the nature and national significance of the American flag, ***Minersville School District, et al v. Gobitis, et al***. [22] The local school board of education, with jurisdiction over the public schools of Minersville, Pennsylvania, required both teachers and pupils to participate in a flag ceremony. The right hand is placed on the breast and the following pledge recited in unison:

> "I pledge allegiance to my flag, and to the Republic for which it stands; one nation indivisible, with liberty and justice for all."

The Gobitis family were affiliated with "Jehovah's Witnesses", for whom the Bible as the Word of God is the supreme authority. The children had been brought up conscientiously to believe that such a gesture of respect for the flag was forbidden by command of scripture. The Gobitis children refused to engage in that ceremony in consequence of which their attendance as students in the public school was terminated. The Gobitis family brought a lawsuit seeking to have the court declare this ceremony policy unconstitutional as constituting an abridgement of their religious beliefs, which they contended were protected by the Fourteenth Amendment. Thus there was presented to the court the right of the people to embody their virtues and opinions in legislation as opposed to the religious freedom of an individual. The gravity of the legal question presented was stated by the Court in these words:

> "A grave responsibility confronts this Court whenever in course of litigation it must reconcile the conflicting claims of liberty and authority. But when the liberty invoked is liberty of conscience, and the authority is authority to safeguard the nation's fellowship, judicial conscience is put to its severest test. Of such a nature is the present controversy."

The court stated the question presented in these words:

> "We must decide whether the requirement of participation in such a ceremony, exacted from a child who refuses upon sincere religious grounds, infringes without due process of law the liberty guaranteed by the Fourteenth Amendment."

In the course of the opinion, authored by Justice Frankfurter, the court affirmatively stated that one's conviction "about the mystery of the universe and man's relation to it is placed beyond the reach of law" and, therefore, government may not interfere with organized or individual expression of belief or disbelief, "whether in church or chapel, mosque, or synagogue, tabernacle or meeting house." This notwithstanding the court took notice of a fact that a citizen's conception of religious duty may come in conflict with the "secular interest of his fellow men, those interests including what society thinks necessary for the promotion of some great common end." Justice Frankfurter then turned his attention to the nature of our democratic society and the national significance of our flag. He observed that our democracy was "an organized political society." Then he affirmed:

> "The ultimate foundation of a free society is the binding tie of cohesive sentiment. Such a sentiment is fostered by all those agencies of the mind and spirit which may serve to gather up the traditions of a people, transmit them from generation to generation, and thereby create that continuity of a treasured common life which constitutes a civilization."

Then Justice Frankfurter addressed the nature and national function of the flag, saying:

> "We live by symbols. The flag is the symbol of our national unity, transcending all internal differences, however large, within the framework of the Constitution. This Court has had occasion to say that " . . . the flag is the symbol of the nation's power, — the emblem of freedom in its truest, best sense. . . . It signifies government resting on the consent of the governed; liberty regulated by law; the protection of the weak against the strong; security

> against the exercise of arbitrary power; and the absolute safety for free institutions against foreign aggression."

The court postulated that there was no dispute as to the genuineness of the religious scruples of the Gobitis family in controversy and as to the purpose of the legislation, whose constitutionality was in contest. The court found that the flag ceremony was an appropriate action "to evoke that unifying sentiment without which there can ultimately be no liberties, civil or religious." It concluded that such an end "is legitimate." The wisdom of training children in patriotic impulses by the school board compulsions in controversy "is not for our independent judgment." And while some may believe that the "deepest patriotism" is best promoted "by giving unfettered scope to the most crotchety beliefs" such rights or conditions fall outside the court room arena. Justice Frankfurter affirmatively stated that it is not the "province" of the court to choose among competing considerations "in the subtle process of securing effective loyalty to the traditional ideals of democracy." The bottom line of the legal question presented called into focus what Lincoln earlier said:

> "Must a government of necessity be too strong for the liberties of its people, or too weak to maintain its own existence?"

Justice Frankfurter summarized the rationale of the decision of the court in reversing the lower court and rejecting the claim of the Gobitis family by declaring:

> "The preciousness of the relation, the authority and independence which give dignity to parenthood, indeed the

> enjoyment of all freedom, presuppose the kind of ordered society which is summarized by our flag. A society which is dedicated to the preservation of these ultimate values of civilization may in self-protection utilize the educational process for inculcating those almost unconscious feelings which bind men together in a comprehending loyalty, whatever may be their lesser differences and difficulties. That is to say, the process may be utilized so long as men's right to believe as they please, to win others to their way of belief, and their right to assemble in their chosen places of worship for the devotional ceremonies of their faith, are all fully respected."

"But to the legislature no less than the courts is committed the guardianship of deeply-cherished liberties", said Justice Frankfurter. Finally the court postulated:

> "To fight out the wise use of legislative authority in the forum of public opinion and before legislative assemblies rather than to transfer such a contest to the judicial arena, serves to vindicate the self-confidence of a free people."

This decision was made, this message of the symbolism of our flag was published on June 3, 1940, almost exactly eighteen (18) months before the infamous attack by the Japanese on Pearl Harbor, which propelled America into World War II. Soldiers on Iwo Jima understood and were inspired by the ideals embodied in our flag and its necessity as a unifying instrument of our free institutions.

However, on June 14, 1943, almost exactly eighteen (18) months after the sneak attack on Pearl Harbor (Dec. 7, 1941), the Supreme Court reversed its decision in the ***Gobitis*** case regarding the American Flag as discussed above, ***West Virginia State Board of Education, et al v. Barnette, et al.*** [23]

Before going into the merits of the ***Barnette*** decision, it will be helpful to point out and discuss several things that are startling about that decision. Firstly, the ***Gobitis*** decision was rendered eighteen months before America became involved as a combatant in World War II. and thus at a time when the tug of patriotism was not activated by the emergency of any imminent threat to our national security by a foreign power. Thus the ***Gobitis*** decision of 1940 was rendered in a political ambience of peace, unimpeded by any passion excited by any national imperative, other than the compelling force to vindicate the ideals of our national life. Secondly, on the other hand, the 1943 ***Barnette*** decision, reversing the 1940 ***Gobitis*** decision, was rendered at a time when we were at war. According to Secretary of the Navy, Knox, it was reported that the sneak attack on Pearl Harbor had resulted in the battleship, Arizona, and the target ship, Utah, being sunk and the battleship, Oklahoma, was capsized, a mine layer and three destroyers sunk, and heavy damage was inflicted on our air force. In February of 1942, President Roosevelt broadcast the Pearl Harbor attack casualties of our American soldiers as 2,340 killed and 946 wounded. Following the Pearl Harbor attack the Japanese appeared off Alaska in the Aleutian Islands. In May 1942 there transpired the naval battle of the Coral Sea which brought about the loss of the aircraft, Lexington. The Marines landed on Guadel Canal. Casualties were daily mounting in alarming proportions. It was during 1942, the year before the Supreme Court rendered its ***Barnette*** decision, reversing the ***Gobitis*** decision concerning the American flag, that America began mobilizing its resources and its industrial output. In the mobilization effort there was imposed rationing of food stuff and gasoline, and intensification of the draft. And for the first time in the history of America women were inducted into the armed services, designated as WAACS, starting with 25,000 women with an ultimate enrollment of 150,000 functioning as an auxiliary army to the war effort. And by this time France had been conquered by Germany. General de Gaulle of France organized a "free France" army in exile in anticipation of returning to France to reverse her conquest. It was in 1942 as well that the traitor, Laval, of France, who had returned to power and influence at Vichy, was trying to provide "full collaboration" of Vichy France with the occupying Nazis. 24

Thus, the 1943 ***Barnette*** decision, reversing the earlier ***Gobitis*** decision, was rendered at a time in our history when the element of patriotism was indispensably needful as the most potent force to confront and repel the all-out attack on our nation and on western civilization. It was at this time and under these circumstances that our Supreme Court declared that our flag, the symbol of our political sacraments, was no longer to be an object of respect or reverence. And the ***Barnette*** decision spawned subsequent decisions, the effect of which was to declare that our flag is nothing but a rag piece to be spat upon, trampled underfoot, burned, and otherwise desecrated with absolute impunity, all to the painful chagrin and discontent of the majority of the peoples of our nation.

This 1943 decision suggests a perilous judicial activism on the part of the majority in the Supreme Court. (Judicial activism in this instance involves the court in usurping the power of the legislature.) How else is the flip-flop of the Supreme Court over the short period of three years regarding a fundamental constitutional question explainable except by judicial activism. A reading of the 1943 ***Barnette*** decision strongly indicates that the majority of the court agreed to reverse the 1940 ***Gobitis*** decision and thereafter went in search of reasons to support that agreement. The process of that 1943 ***Barnette*** decision engaged the court in eschewing and avoiding the application of the standard of review ordained by the original intent of the founders of our democratic ideals.

A brief visit to the paradigm or the rule of interpretation to which our Constitution commits the Supreme Court will be helpful in realizing the court's departure from that rule in deciding the ***Barnette*** case. It will be remembered that the paradigm contemplates a critical analysis by the court of any legislation involved in controversy to determine if it "secures the general comfort, health and prosperity of the state" and its people. In reaching such a conclusion the court must then give effect to the majority rule and thereby permit the political views and opinions of the people to be embodied in permissible legislation. This paradigm of construction provides that on reaching such a conclusion that the legislation does secure the welfare of our people then that rule gives effect to the constitutional calculus that "all kinds of restraints and burdens" must be endured by the citizens "in order to secure the general" welfare of society. The 1943 ***Barnette*** court, however, studiously avoided application and implementation of that rule of judicial interpretation.

The 1943 ***Barnette*** case involved the enforcement of a pledge of allegiance to our flag essentially identical with the 1940 ***Gobitis*** case. The pledge involved in the ***Barnette*** case is as follows:

> "I pledge allegiance to the flag of the United States of America and to the republic for which it stands; one nation, indivisible, with liberty and justice for all."

At the very beginning of the opinion of the court it affirmed that the ***Barnette*** case "calls upon us to reconsider" the ***Gobitis*** case. The court observed that the "sole conflict" in the case was "between authority and the rights of the individual". Further the court stated that this compulsory flag salute and pledge "requires affirmation of a belief and an attitude of mind". In avoiding a discussion of the public good of this pledge, the court simply stated that the privilege of the First Amendment was not "dependent upon whether as a voluntary exercise we would think it to be good, bad or merely innocuous". Building upon this postulation the court avoided any discussion of the good of the pledge of allegiance involved. The court refused to deal with the ringing words of Justice Frankfurter in the Gobitis case when he said:

> "The preciousness of the relation, the authority and independence which give dignity to parenthood, indeed the enjoyment of all freedom, presuppose the kind of ordered society which is summarized by <u>our flag</u>. A society which is dedicated to the preservation of these ultimate values of civilization may in self-protection utilize the educational process for inculcating those almost unconscious feelings which bind men together in a comprehending loyalty, whatever may be their lesser differences and difficulties. That is to say, the process may be utilized so long as men's right to believe as they please, to win others to their way of belief, and their right to assemble in their chosen places of worship for the devotional ceremonies of their faith, are all fully respected."

Instead, the 1943 ***Barnette*** court said that what was presented to the court in the ***Barnette*** case were:

> "questions of **power** that must be considered **independently** of any idea that we may have as to the utility of the ceremony in question".

First, that statement reflects sophistry at its best. It is superficially plausible, but actually fallacious. And this fallacious statement constitutes the linchpin of the ultimate decision of the majority. This method of argument is characterized by the aristotelian technique of defining the object of the controversy by naming a genus of the controversy friendly to the ultimate goal of the majority. And having selected a fallacious genus, the majority then proceeded to unravel it to its full logical extension. The fallacious genus trumpeted by the majority consists of the court's statement that what was presented to the court were "questions of power". That statement is fallacious because the court has no constitutional jurisdiction to assess the "power" of the Texas Legislature and here is why.

First, the structure of government consists of three branches, the legislative, judicial and executive. The legislative branch is exclusively empowered to make our laws, the judicial branch of government is exclusively empowered to determine the validity or constitutionality of any law passed by the legislative branch, and the executive branch is exclusively empowered to implement and enforce our laws. Neither of these branches of government may intrude upon the other. The majority in this case violated the structural integrity of our system of government by assigning to itself the constitutional jurisdiction to speak to the "power" of the legislative branch of government. Such an intrusion betrays a lack of respect for our fundamental system of government and amounts to legal heresy.

Second, the "power" of the state legislature to enact the law in controversy additionally exists in the Tenth Amendment of the United States Constitution. We must remember at this point of our discussion that our national government is a government of delegated powers, power delegated to it by the several states. All powers not delegated remain with the states. The Tenth Amendment provides:

> "The powers not delegated to the United States by the Constitution, nor prohibited by it to the states, are reserved to the states respectively or <u>to the people</u>."

It was in the exercise of that reserved "power" that the state of Texas enacted the law in controversy. To question and/or diminish that reserved "power" is to violate the provisions of the Tenth Amendment.

Thirdly, the court may not assess the constitutionality of any law without first deciding whether or not such a law is reasonably calculated to "secure the rights of the people". In other words, whether or not the Pledge of Allegiance as part of the educational process was an appropriate device for "inculcating those almost unconscious feelings which bind men together in a comprehending loyalty" is a constitutional proposition that the 1943 ***Barnette*** court was compelled to address. But it avoided that obligation by considering the "power" of the legislative branch of government "independently of any idea that we may have as to thc utility of the ceremony in question". Thus having created its own formula of interpretation, it was with much ease that the 1943 ***Barnette*** court concluded that the state had no such "power".

Fourthly, the majority opinion is fatally flawed for yet another reason. The wisdom of the legislation in question is to be exclusively determined by the legislature. As Justice Frankfurter stated in the ***Gobitis*** case such legislation must have its origin in the legislative process, there to be debated as to the wisdom or need of such legislation. Remember Justice Frankfurter's statement in ***Gobitis***:

> "To fight out the wise use of legislative authority in the forum of public opinion and before legislative assemblies rather than to transfer such a contest to the judicial arena, serves to vindicate the self-confidence of a free people."

Fifthly, Justice Frankfurter in the ***Barnette*** case reminded the majority that:

> "The only check upon our exercise of power is our own sense of self-restraint. For the removal of unwise laws from the statute books appeal lies not to the court but to the ballot and to the processes of democratic government."

Thus the disregard of that moral constraint instances a judicial moral decline. The ***Gobitis*** decision quoted what Lincoln had said:

> "Must a government of necessity be too strong for the liberties of its people, or too weak to maintain its own existence?"

The 1940 ***Gobitis*** court opted for strength rather than weakness. The 1943 ***Barnette*** court disposed of Lincoln's dilemma by gratuitously offering that Lincoln would not have reached the same conclusion as did the 1940 ***Gobitis*** court. The 1943 ***Barnette*** case offered yet another constitutional formula that would endure for years and inflict upon the people of America grievous distress, discontent and alienation of the people from their government. This new formula was verbalized by the ***Barnette*** court in these words:

> "The subject now before us exemplifies this principle. Free public education, if faithful to the ideal of secular instruction and **POLITICAL NEUTRALITY**, will not be partisan or enemy of any class, creed, party, or faction. If it is to impose any ideological discipline, however, each party or denomination must seek to control, or failing that, **to weaken the influence of the educational system**." . . .

The foregoing statement instances extremism in the defense of nothing but power. How can our schools teach what our ideals of government are, if a teacher must maintain "political neutrality"? Our schools are the intellectual nurseries of the very young and the maturing young students. The students are the beneficiaries of caring teachers dedicated to informing their minds to the need of knowledge as an instrument to understand the world about them, past and present; and to excite in them an intellectual curiosity regarding the dynamics of moral and ethical rectitude, of human dignity, of intellectual honesty, of the concept of ordered liberty, of the virtue of self discipline, and of the nature and significance of an ordered society in order to equip them to make reliable decisions as to their personal lives, their association with others, and as to the fundamental values of our system of government. This is the stuff which creates "belief and an attitude of mind". If such teaching should not be done in our schools, then where else! In bar rooms? At the feet of drug gurus? On the streets as members of predatory gangs?

Furthermore, the court's statement above mentioned advocates not only disrespect for the law but invites insidious rebellion against the law by the people. As that statement reflects, the court urges that if a party cannot "control" the educational system in its teaching regarding our national existence, then the party must "weaken the influence of the educational system". The term "weaken" is of such a generic nature that it includes destroying the educational system. As will appear on the following pages, this concept of "neutrality" was to become the handmaiden of the court in avoiding the assessment of a variety of actions and speech in the area of public order, personal responsibility and public decency.

The Dissents

This case is a mother lode of American constitutionalism. It is a dramatic debate over contrasting views of our democracy by men of great learning and diction. It brings into sharp focus the concepts of the origin of power, the conflict between the majority and minority rights, the role of religion in our political government, the limiting nature of the Bill of Rights, and the separation of power of our national character.

Three justices dissented from the majority opinion: Mr. Justice Frankfurter, who wrote the opinion in the ***Gobitis*** case, Mr. Justice Roberts and Mr. Justice Reed. Mr. Justice Frankfurter gave extensive reasons for his dissent. A reference to some of his reasons gives to we the people the opportunity better to evaluate the acceptability of the majority opinion. At the outset, Justice Frankfurter reminded that he was a Jew, and as such he, "belongs to the most vilified and persecuted minority in history". If his duties called upon him to express his personal opinion, he would join the majority. But then he said:

"But as judges we are neither Jew nor Gentile, neither

> Catholic nor agnostic. We owe equal attachment to the Constitution and are equally bound by our judicial obligations whether we derive our citizenship from the earliest or the latest immigrants to these shores. As a member of this Court I am not justified in writing my private notions of policy into the Constitution, no matter how deeply I may cherish them or how mischievous I may deem their disregard."

Then he pointed out that the majority decision, to the effect that the sole question presented to the court was one of **"power"** of the legislature, existed in violation of the separation of power of our political structure because it engaged the majority in usurping the power of the legislature and substituting its judgment of the wisdom of their legislation.

Justice Frankfurter further stated that all that is in question [in this case] is the right of the state to compel participation in this exercise [flag ceremony] by those who choose to attend the public schools. Further he said:

> "Under our constitutional system the legislature is charged solely with civil concerns of society.
>
> . . . . .
>
> A court can only strike down. It can only say 'This or that law is void'. It cannot modify or qualify, it cannot make exceptions to a general requirement."

In commenting upon the constitutional protection of religious freedom, Justice Frankfurter said:

> "The constitutional protection of religious freedom terminated disabilities, it did not create new privilege. It gave religious equality, **not civil immunity**. Its essence is freedom from conformity to religious dogma, **not freedom from conformity to law** because of religious dogma. Religious loyalties may be exercised without hindrance from the state, nor the state may not exercise that which except by leave of religious loyalties is within the domain of temporal power. Otherwise each individual could set up his own censor against obedience to laws conscientiously deemed for the public good by those whose business it is to make laws."

Noting that as of 1943 there were more than 250 "distinctive established religious denominations" in the United States, 120 of which existed in the state of Pennsylvania and 65 in the state of West Virginia, he stated:

> "But the lawmaking authority is not circumscribed by the variety of religious beliefs, otherwise the constitutional guaranty would be not a protection of the free exercise of religion but a denial of the exercise of legislation."
>
> . . . . .
>
> But an act promoting good citizenship and national allegiance is within the domain of governmental authority and is therefore to be judged by the same considerations

> of power and of constitutionality as those involved in the many claims of immunity from civil obedience because of religious scruples."

Justice Frankfurter made the further observation that the effect of the majority rule "really means that the consciences of a minority are more sacred and more enshrined in the Constitution than the consciences of a majority".

In the majority opinion was mentioned that a salute was comparable to saluting Hitler. In response to that, Justice Frankfurter said:

> "And surely only flippancy could be responsible for the suggestion that our constitutional validity of a requirement to salute our flag implies equal validity of a requirement to salute a dictator. The significance of a symbol lies in what it represents. To reject the swastika does not imply rejection of the Cross.
>
> . . . . .
>
> To deny the power to employ educational symbols is to say that the state's educational system may not stimulate the imagination because this may lead to unwise stimulation."

In commenting upon the flip-flop of the court regarding a grave constitutional question over a period of three years, Justice Frankfurter said:

> "We are dealing with matters as to which legislators and

> voters have conflicting views. Are we as judges to impose our strong convictions on where wisdom lies? That which three years ago had seemed to five successive Courts to lie within permissible areas of legislation is now outlawed by the deciding shift of opinion of two Justices. What reason is there to believe that they or their successors may not have another view a few years hence? Is that which was deemed to be of so fundamental a nature as to be written into the Constitution to endure for all times to be the sport of shifting winds of doctrine?"

After criticizing the majority for substituting their view of the wisdom of the legislation for that of the legislature, Justice Frankfurter appropriately observed:

> "If the function of this Court is to be essentially no different from that of a legislature, if the considerations governing constitutional construction are to be substantially those that underlie legislation, then indeed judges should not have life tenure and they should be made directly responsible to the electorate."

Finally Justice Frankfurter postulated:

> "We are told that a flag salute is a doubtful substitute for adequate understanding of our institutions. The states that require such a school exercise do not have to justify it as the only means for promoting good citizenship in children, but merely as one of diverse means for accomplishing a worthy end. We may deem it a foolish measure, but

the point is that this Court is not the organ of government to resolve doubts as to whether it will fulfill its purpose. Only if there be no doubt that any reasonable mind could entertain can we deny to the states the right to resolve doubts their way and not ours."

Then Justice Frankfurter asserted the following peroration:

"Of course patriotism cannot be enforced by the flag salute. But neither can the liberal spirit be enforced by judicial invalidation of illiberal legislation. Our constant preoccupation with the constitutionality of legislation rather than with its wisdom tends to preoccupation of the American mind with a false value. The tendency of focusing attention on constitutionality is to make constitutionality synonymous with wisdom, to regard a law as all right if it is constitutional. Such an attitude is a great enemy of liberalism. Particularly in legislation affecting freedom of thought and freedom of speech much which should offend a free-spirited society is constitutional. Reliance for the most precious interests of civilization, therefore, must be found outside of their vindication in courts of law. Only a persistent positive translation of the faith of a free society into the convictions and habits and actions of a community is the ultimate reliance against unabated temptations to fetter the human spirit."

As earlier stated, this case places on display the essential values of our system of government in contrasting dialogues. We the people can decide for ourselves which of the contrasting views identify with our feeling of what is best for we the people. While in the process of the decision-making effort certain fundamental precepts must frame the outer contour of that decision. At bottom is the Constitutional command that the power of our government, state and federal, originates with we the people. This command implicates the following political truth: Nothing exists in our laws which did not first exist in we the people. And thus it is that our sense of civic virtue and individual responsibility are the nutrients of our collective ideals. Our national anthem, the soul of our nation, is all about our flag. Interestingly enough, our 1998 Congress has initiated the adoption of a resolution to amend our Constitution to protect our flag against desecration. What a propitious moment in our history for self-expression.

The 1943 ***Barnette*** decision created much public consternation. In time of war, while our soldiers were making the supreme sacrifice, and where the flag, affectionately known as "Old Glory", was a daily companion symbolically uniting our soldiers with their comrades and with the loved ones left behind, the Supreme Court declared that Old Glory was unworthy of compulsory acknowledgment and respect. The public could not understand how it was that our Constitution, with all of its reach for God and its ideals enshrining human dignity, compelled the degradation of our flag in which our nation is wrapped, as the ***Barnette*** court did. Additionally the public was concerned that such a decision would adversely affect the morale of our soldiers. Uncannily a state of future shock resonated among our people throughout America. The dastardly notion settled upon them that the degradation of our flag by the ***Barnette*** court opened the door to future flag desecration. By 1989, 52 years after the ***Barnette*** decision was rendered, with the exception of

Alaska and Wyoming, every state had adopted legislation making it a criminal offense to desecrate our flag. Nevertheless the people's sense of future shock became an agonizing reality on June 21, 1989 when the Supreme Court decided the case of ***Texas v. Johnson***.[25] This was a six to three decision.

While the Republican National Convention was taking place in Dallas in 1984, one Gregory Lee Johnson, participated in a political demonstration dubbed the "Republic War Chest Tour". The purpose of the demonstration was to protest the policies of the Reagan Administration and of certain Dallas-based corporations. These protestors stopped in front of certain corporate offices to stage a "die-ins". On several occasions the court said that they "spray painted the walls of buildings and overturned potted plants". While Johnson did not participate in those activities he did however, "accept an American flag handed to him by a fellow protestor who had taken it from a flag pole outside one of the targeted buildings". While in front of the Dallas City Hall Johnson "unfurled the American flag, doused it with kerosene and set it on fire". And while the flag burned, these protestors chanted "America, the red, white and blue we spit on you". Following the disbursal of the demonstrators a witness to the flag burning "collected the flag's remains and buried them in his back yard". Johnson was thereafter charged by the State of Texas with a violation of a Texas statute which prohibited the "desecration of a venerated object", the flag. The Supreme Court stated what it believed to be the issue before the court:

> "Johnson was convicted of flag desecration for burning the flag rather than for uttering insulting words. This fact somewhat complicates our consideration of his conviction under the First Amendment."

The court concluded that "Johnson's burning of the flag constituted expressive conduct, permitting him to invoke the First Amendment and challenging his conviction". In reaching such a conclusion there must be the presence of "an intent to convey a particularized message . . . and the likelihood was great that the message would be understood by those who viewed it". Ironically the majority opinion acknowledges that "the flag's salute is a form of utterance . . . the use of an emblem or flag to symbolize some system, idea, institution or personality, is a shortcut from mind to mind". It follows from that statement that the saluting of the flag is a communication instancing the approval and embracing of what America stands for and is therefore, necessarily protected by the First Amendment of free speech. Notably, however, the Supreme Court gave no consideration to the right of we the people under the First Amendment. During the course of the opinion, the majority affirmed that:

> "A law directed at the communicative nature of conduct must, like a law directed at speech itself, be justified by the substantial showing of need that the First Amendment requires."

In such a case, it is the "governmental interest at stake that helps to determine whether a restriction on that expression is valid". In formulating the foundation for its ultimate decision the court stated that:

> "Function of free speech under our system of government is to invite dispute. It may indeed best serve its high purpose when it induces a condition of unrest, creates dissatisfaction with the conditions as they are, or even stirs people to anger."

The court then concluded that the state statute forbidding the desecration of the flag was unconstitutional because it denied Johnson's First Amendment right of free speech. In rationalizing that conclusion the Court said:

> "And, precisely because it is our flag that is involved, one's response to the flag burner may exploit the uniquely persuasive power of the flag itself. We can imagine no more appropriate response to burning a flag than waving one's own, no better way to counter a flag burner's message than by saluting the flag that burns, no surer means of preserving the dignity even of the flag that burned than by — as one witness here did — according its remains a respectful burial. We do not consecrate the flag by punishing its desecration, for in doing so we dilute the freedom that this cherished emblem represents."

It is a good investment of time to pause long enough to closely scrutinize this statement of the court. That statement affirms that the use of the flag to protest or support governmental policy constitutes a species of speech protected by the First Amendment of the Constitution. Flag saluting, therefore, is a *speech* supportive of our government policies functioning as a unifying agency of we the people. Flag burning is a *speech* protesting our government policies, functioning as an agency to divide the people of America. If both speeches are protected by the First Amendment, then how can the speech of one individual seeking to promote division be declared more sacred than the speech of the overwhelming majority of we the people? If the flag embodies the ideals of our system of government, then it follows that the majority of our people have the legitimate duty to protect our flag against desecration and/or destruction, since the flag is an integral part of speech. This decision engages the court in violating the original intent of our Constitution. It engages the court in reversing the concept of the original intent of the Constitution in that it makes the right of the individual superior to the right of the people.

In rendering this decision the court has now gone full circle and got in bed with the 1897 - 1937 court by resurrecting the discarded constitutional notion that individual rights trump the rights of we the people. The devil in the law advocating such an inverted priority of rights was thought duly buried by the 1937 decision of the court in the ***Parrish*** case. Now we see by this notable decision the disinterment of this devil and the giving of an applauding shot in the arm to cast on the ash heap of history the fundamental concept that the majority of we the people must prevail in the enactment of legislation legitimately designed to promote and protect the health, comfort and welfare of the people.

The Dissent

Justice Rehnquist began his dissent by affirming that the majority had ignored Justice Holmes' familiar aphorism that "a page of history is worth a volume of logic". Further, he declared that:

> "For more than 200 years the American flag has occupied the unique position as the symbol of our Nation, a uniqueness that justifies a governmental prohibition against flag burning in the way respondent Johnson did here."

He outlined a litany of historic uses made of our flag since its adoption. He alluded to the War of 1812 at a time when British naval forces sailed up Chesapeake Bay on their way to Baltimore, but it was necessary for these forces to reduce Fort McHenry in Baltimore Harbor. Francis Scott Key, a Washington lawyer, who had been granted permission by the British to negotiate the release of an American who had been taken prisoner that night waited anxiously and watched the British fleet firing on Fort McHenry. Finally at daybreak he saw the fort's American flag still flying. "Intensely moved, he began to scribble on the back of an envelope the poem that became our national anthem", said Justice Rehnquist. He confirmed that the flag is placed at half mast in honor of officials, traditionally placed on the casket of deceased members of the armed forces and later given to the deceased's family. In 1949 Congress declared June 14th to be Flag Day; Congress established "The Pledge of Allegiance to the Flag" and the manner of its deliverance. Finally he pointed to the law adopted by Congress which provides:

> "Whoever knowingly casts contempt upon any flag of the United States by publicly mutilating, defacing, defiling, burning, or trampling upon it shall be fined not more than $1,000 or imprisoned for not more than one year, or both."

He responded to the majority opinion that this Texas law infringed upon Johnson's freedom of expression by simply observing that "such freedom, of course, is not absolute". He then approvingly referred to a 1942 decision of the Supreme Court in ***Chaplinsky v. New Hampshire*** [26] in which by a unanimous court said:

> "Allowing the broadest scope to the language and purpose of the Fourteenth Amendment, it is well understood that the right of free speech is **not absolute** at all times and under all circumstances. There are certain well-de-

> fined and narrowly limited classes of speech, the prevention and punishment of which have never been thought to raise any Constitutional problem. These include the **lewd** and **obscene**, the **profane**, the **libelous** and the **insulting** or 'fighting' words — those which **by their very utterance inflict injury or tend to incite an immediate breach of the peace**. It has been well observed that such utterances are no essential part of any exposition of ideas, and are of **such slight social value** as a step to truth that any benefit that may be derived from them is **clearly outweighed by the social interest in order and morality**?"

Justice Rehnquist observed that the burning of the flag "had a tendency to incite a breach of the peace". At all times during Johnson's protest no one interfered with his right to free speech, and the State of Texas did not initiate any prosecution regarding his speech. His speech was loud and vitriolic, shouting out slogans such as:

> "Reagan, Mondale which will it be? Either one means World War III."
>
> Ronald Reagan, killer of the hour, perfect example of U. S. power."
>
> "Red, white and blue, we spit on you, you stand for plunder, you will go under."

Then Justice Rehnquist observed:

> "For none of these acts was he arrested or prosecuted; it was only when he proceeded to burn publicly an American flag **stolen** from its rightful owner that he violated the Texas statute."

Justice Rehnquist dismissed the notion that flag burning could be equivalent to the aphorism that "one picture being worth a thousand words". Instead Justice Rehnquist stated:

> "Flag burning is the equivalent of an inarticulate grunt or roar that, it seems fair to say, is most likely to be indulged in not to express any particular idea, but to antagonize others."

He made reference to former Chief Justice Warren's dissent in an earlier case where Justice Warren stated:

> "I believe that the States and Federal Government do have the power to protect the flag from acts of desecration and disgrace . . . [I]t is difficult for me to imagine that, had the Court faced this issue, it would have concluded otherwise."

Justice Rehnquist also referred to earlier comments of former Justices Black and Fortas, quoting approvingly what Justice Black said:

> "It passes my belief that anything in the Federal Constitution bars a State from making the deliberate burning of the American Flag an offense."

And quoted from Justice Fortas his comment:

> "[T]he States and the Federal Government have the power

> to protect the flag from acts of desecration committed in public . . . [T]he flag is a special kind of personality. Its use is traditionally and universally subject to special rules and regulation . . .A person may 'own' a flag, but ownership is subject to special burdens and responsibilities . . ."

Justice Rehnquist made the following analogous comparison when he said that:

> "There would seem to be little question about the power of Congress to forbid mutilation of the Lincoln Memorial . . .. The flag is itself a monument."

In criticizing the majority for stating that the people's deep awe and respect for the flag fell under the rubric of "designated symbols", Justice Rehnquist said that the government did not establish such a symbol, instead:

> "200 years of history have done that. The government is simply recognizing as a fact the profound regard for the American flag created by that history when it enacts statutes prohibiting the disrespectful public burning of the flag."

After making a general allusion to the Revolutionary War with England and in singling out that the controlling reasons for our independence was "no taxation without representation", Justice Rehnquist stated that such a notion grants to the governed some say as to what kind of laws would be passed:

> "Surely one of the high purposes of a democratic society

> is to legislate against conduct that is regarded as evil and profoundly offensive to the majority of people — whether it be murder, embezzlement, pollution, or flag burning."

Justice Rehnquist said he would uphold the Texas statute as applied in this case and as additional support for that statement he observed the irony created by the majority opinion in these words:

> "The government may conscript men into the Armed Forces where they must fight and perhaps die for the flag, but the government may not prohibit the public burning of the banner under which they fight."

Justice Stevens, dissenting, pointed out that our country's flag is a symbol of more than "nationhood and national unity". Said he:

> "It also signifies the ideas that characterize the society that has chosen that emblem as well as the special history that has animated the growth and power of those ideas.
>
> . . .
>
> It is more than a proud symbol of the courage, the determination, and the gifts of nature that transformed 13 fledgling Colonies into a world power. It is a symbol of freedom, of equal opportunity, of religious tolerance, and of good will for other peoples who share our aspirations. The symbol carries its message to dissidents both at home and abroad who may have no interest at all in our national unity or survival."

Justice Stevens further reasoned that the majority decision is fraught with the implication that soon there will arise a federal right "to post bulletin boards and graffiti on the Washington Monument" as an expression of free speech. But, said Justice Stevens, "I would not pay" that price in the interest of such unbridled expression. Moreover Justice Steven said "sanctioning the public desecration of a flag will tarnish its value — both for those who cherish the ideas for which it waves and for those who desire to don the robes of martyrdom by burning it". Said Justice Stevens:

> "That tarnish is not justified by the trivial burden on free expression occasioned by requiring that an available, alternative mode of expression — including uttering words critical of the flag be employed."

He stated that the majority was "quite wrong" in asserting that Johnson was prosecuted for his dissatisfaction with "the policies of this country". Justice Stevens said that he was prosecuted not because of what he said but "because of the method he chose to express his dissatisfaction with those policies". He further postulated that had Johnson chosen to spray-paint his message of dissatisfaction on the "facade of the Lincoln Memorial" there can never be any question about the power of the government to prohibit this means of expression. Continuing Justice Stevens said:

> "The prohibition would be supported by the legitimate interest in preserving the quality of an important national asset. Though the asset at stake in this case is intangible, given its unique value, the same interest supports a prohibition on the desecration of the American flag."

Justice Stevens summarized his dissent in these words:

> "The ideas of liberty and equality have been an irresistible force in motivating leaders like Patrick Henry, Susan B. Anthony, and Abraham Lincoln, schoolteachers like Nathan Hale and Booker T. Washington, the Philippine Scouts who fought at Bataan, and the soldiers who scaled the bluff at Omaha Beach. If those ideas are worth fighting for — and our history demonstrates that they are — it cannot be true that the flag that uniquely symbolizes their power is not itself worthy of protection from unnecessary desecration."

And with the plunder of our flag in the juridical war zone came the displacement of the unifying sentiments which our flag inspired, so typically exemplified by the following poetic speech:

"**S**hoot if you must, this old grey head,
But spare your country's flag, she said."[27]

"**A**y, tear her tattered ensign down!
Long has it waved on high,
And many an eye has danced to see
That banner in the sky."[28]

"**F**ling out, fling out, with cheer and shout,
To all the winds Our Country's Banner!
Be every bar, and every star,
Displayed in full and glorious manner!"[29]

"**H**ats off!
Along the street there comes
A blare of bugles, a ruffle of drums,
A flash of color beneath the sky:
Hats off!
The flag is passing by!

Blue and crimson and white it shines
Over the steel-tipped, ordered lines.
Hats off! The colors before us fly
But more than the flag is passing by.

Sea-fights and land-fights, grim and great,
Fought to make and to save the State:
Weary marches and sinking ships;
Cheers of victory on dying lips;

Days of plenty and years of peace;
March of a strong land's swift increase;
Equal justice, right and law,
Stately honor and reverend awe;

Sign of a nation, great and strong
To ward her people from foreign wrong:
Pride and glory and honor, — all
Live in the colors to stand or fall.

Hats off! Along the street there comes

A blare of bugles, a ruffle of drums;
And loyal hearts are beating high:
Hats off! The flag is passing by!"[30]

If the 1998 congressional initiative is successful to amend the Constitution to authorize criminal prosecution for the desecration of our flag, then at the time of ratification, we the people, in voting, will have the last word as to what the flag means and should mean to us.

CHAPTER SIX

A CONCEPTION OF LIBERTY

THE EARLY SEEDBED OF RADICAL LIBERALISM

The conception of liberty under our Constitution involves the balancing of the rights of the individual and the authority of the state. The framework for deciding this balance consists of the philosophy of our system of government. The cardinal principles of that philosophy are (1) political equality among our people; (2) that life, liberty and the pursuit of happiness are endowed by our Creator, as unalienable rights, and exist independently of government, or exist prior to government; and (3) that the majority is to prevail in all matters regarding laws which fulfill the conception of the good life. In speaking to the rights of the individual Justice Field in the ***Slaughterhouse*** case affirmatively stated that these rights were of divine origin "**rights which are the gift of the Creator; which the law does not confer but only recognizes**".

It is helpful to remember the decisions of the court from 1897 to

1937 whereby the rights of the person trumped the rights of the majority of our people. Relying on the rubric of "freedom of contract" the court during that time period denied to the overwhelming majority of the people their right to protect the health and welfare of the laboring element of society. The 1943 ***Barnette*** decision regarding flag saluting ceremony signaled a return to the constitutional philosophy that the right of the person is superior to the right of a majority of the people regarding any legislation that sought to promote and protect what was good for the whole of America.

It is helpful at this point to establish the legal backdrop against which the future decisions of the court are to be silhouetted. Firstly, the unalienable right of the individual is not absolute. Secondly, because of that and before any decision is made as to the right of the individual, the court must determine whether or not the legislation under consideration "secures the general comfort, health and prosperity of the state." If it does, then the right of the individual exists in a subordinate legal position to the right of the majority of the people. And as repeatedly stated by the court, where it is perceived that the proposed legislation is for the good of the whole of our people, then individuals must expect "all kinds of restraints and burdens" on their rights in order to secure the well-being of society.

It was only a matter of time when the court, in the exercise of theoretical sophistry and semanticism, would construct an interpretative device that would preclude any consideration of the will of the majority as a vital, major component of our democracy. In other words, the will of the majority in matters of morals, ethics, speech and religion would be encapsulated in an impenetrable cocoon of "neutrality" as an interpretative device by the court to preclude any judicial consideration of the conception of the good life or morality or goal of any legislation enacted by the majority of the people. This procedure was to engage the court in "bracketing" such issues, and thereby placing beyond the traditional reach of the court, the substantive values of such issues involved in the legislation being considered by the court. And such a procedure represents the reversal of the Jeffersonian constitutional principle that the majority will of the people "shall prevail" and that this constitutional principle was to be determined "with the best light we can obtain on the subject and to administer it as we find it, according to **its true intent and meaning [of the Constitution] when it was adopted**". So declared the Dred Scott case.

Rumblings in the womb of time of what was to come were vaguely discernible but not then definable. Intentionally or unwittingly, some justices of the court verbalized the seminal seed which later was to be utilized to give dominion to the rights of a person over the rights of the majority of the people. An early example occurred in the case of ***Truax v. Corrigan*** (1921).[31] That case involved the right of union laborers to strike and to induce third persons to refuse to do business with their employer, commonly known as a secondary boycott. The majority of the court held that such conduct was illegal and could be enjoined. Justice Holmes, an icon of the judiciary, dissented. In so doing, he intoned:

> "I must add one general consideration. There is **nothing** that I more deprecate than the use of the Fourteenth Amendment beyond the absolute compulsion of its words to **prevent** the making of social experiments that an important part of the community desires . . . even though the experiments may seem **futile** or even **noxious** to me and to those whose judgment I must respect."

Though Justice Holmes' statement was made in defense of the right of the state to enact the legislation under constitutional attack, it was adumbrative of the moral chaos that would later infect the administration of justice as a flesh-eating legal virus.

Close scrutiny of Justice Holmes' statement discloses its tie to subsequent court decisions exemplifying the denial of the right of the people. Justice Holmes was saying that the Fourteenth Amendment could not be invoked to prevent "social experiments" desired by an important part of the community "even though the experiments may seem futile or even **noxious** to me." We must all concede that Justice Holmes was a man of letters, learned and well informed. Therefore he was aware of the meaning of the words which he selected to express his view. The word **noxious**, according to Webster's New Dictionary, means "to hurt, injure; harmful to health; morally injurious; corrupting; unwholesome." Wittingly or not Justice Holmes proclaimed that morally injurious, corrupting, and injurious health action, speech or conduct could not be prevented by the Constitution, implying that he favored a laissez-faire morality, to freely roam about the societal fabric of personal rectitude. For example if a state should enact legislation condemning certain conduct as corrupting the morals of our people, according to Holmes' perception of his duty, he would "bracket" or remain "neutral" as to the moral content of such a law. Such "neutrality" would exempt him from considering and deciding the conception of good or the corruption of the intrinsic morality of such a law, leaving him to decide only the question of whether one violating this law was denied of Due Process, a procedural right, that is, essentially a right to be heard. As will appear later this "content neutrality"or "bracketing" device robs the majority of the people of the right to determine the precepts of morality and ethics thought more suitable to the conception of the good life on behalf of the majority.

Another example of Justice Holmes' expansive view of the individual's rights under the Bill of Rights occurs in the case of ***Gitlow v. People of the State of New York** (1923).* [32] Gitlow was indicted for allegedly violating the New York statutory crime of "criminal anarchy". He was tried and convicted. The state's statute provided that criminal anarchy "is the doctrine that organized government should be overthrown by force or violence, or by assassination of the executive head or of any of the executive officials of government, or by unlawful means". The charge against Gitlow was that he had advocated and advised the overthrow of government by force, violence and unlawful means. This advocacy of the overthrow of government consisted of a writing entitled ***"The Left Wing Manifesto"***, printed, published and knowingly circulated by Gitlow. The Supreme Court agreed that Gitlow was advocating the violent overthrow of organized government. The court noted the purpose of this overthrow, quoting from the Manifesto:

> "The proletariat revolution and the Communist reconstruction of society - the struggle for these - is now dispensable . . .. The Communist International calls the proletariat of the world to the final struggle."

The defendant contended that such a law infringed his right of free speech as guaranteed by the First Amendment and due process clause of the Constitution. The court concluded that actions of advocating the overthrow of organized government "in their essential nature are inherently unlawful in a constitutional government of law and order". And in rejecting Gitlow's claim to freedom of speech the court held:

> "It is a fundamental principle, long established, that the freedom of speech and of the press which is secured by the Constitution, does **not** confer an **absolute right** to speak or publish, without responsibility, whatever one may choose, or an unrestricted and unbridled license that gives immunity for every possible use of language and prevents the punishment of those who abuse this freedom."

Further, the court affirmed that "reasonably limited" freedom of speech "is an inestimable privilege in a free government." But, said the court, "without such limitation, it might become the scourge of the republic." The court further affirmed that a state may punish "utterances endangering the foundations of organized government and threatening its overthrow by unlawful means." Freedom of speech and press does not protect one against "the attempt to subvert the government." Responding to Gitlow's complaint that there was no evidence to show that his speech had incited violence the court dismissed that by simply saying:

> "A single revolutionary spark may kindle a fire that, smoldering for a time, may burst into a sweeping and destructive conflagration."

The Supreme Court then affirmed the conviction of Gitlow. Justice Holmes dissented joined by Justice Brandeis. The essence of his dissent is his expansive view of the Fourteenth Amendment and due process. It was his view that the First Amendment of free speech protected one who advocates the overthrow of our government. He verbalized his concept of free speech in the following words:

> "If in the long run the beliefs expressed in proletarian dictatorship are destined to be accepted by the dominant forces of the community, the only meaning of the free speech is that they should be given their chance and have their way."

Such a statement of free speech is constitutionally disturbing, if not alarming. It is certainly true that we the people, where governmental power originates, by voting, may amend our Constitution or even repeal it; and simultaneously adopt a constitution authorizing and providing for a "proletarian dictatorship." But the power to do so is beyond the jurisdictional reach of the Supreme Court. That court is without jurisdictional reach to amend the Constitution either under the guise of interpreting it in such a manner as to effect an insidious erosion of the fundamental principles of self-government, or by arbitrary and overt decision to the effect that the Constitution is itself unconstitutional.

Justice Holmes had great verbal skills. He could reduce a profound philosophy of government into a simple, but explicit, metaphorical statement. And this he did, reflecting his judicial philosophy as a judge, in a letter (now quite famous) to his friend, Harold Lasky. His famous statement was "If my fellow citizens want to go to hell I will help them. It's my job." Surely he must have been in an expansive mood when he made that statement. And probably intended it as rhetoric. But then who knows. After all, in the ***Gitlow*** case he thought that advocating the violent overthrow of our government was speech protected by our Constitution. And that constitutional protection would enable one citizen, advocating the violent overthrow of our government, to permissibly establish a dictatorship, if he were able to convince the people of the preferential worth of a dictatorship.

Holmes' statement has both humor and danger. To understand this is to understand that "hell" is universally defined as a place of punishment for the wicked after death; the abode of evil souls. The humor is that Justice Holmes considered his duty as a judge to help the wicked go to hell. The danger is that this implies that the wicked exists on a constitutional level even with those members of society who support government by exercising civic virtues. And for those who may wish to read into his statement that wicked conduct will be sanctioned by the court, such a statement is at war with one of the most fundamental principles of our philosophy of government. As earlier stated our government rests upon the proclamation that God exists and that he has endowed our people with certain unalienable rights. Any claim by a citizen to want to go to "hell" is found in no existing law. Such a claim seemingly is not one among the unalienable rights of citizens, because an "unalienable" right is "the gift of the Creator", as the court said in the ***Slaughterhouse*** case. To sustain that view, as reflected in Holmes' statement, one would have to conclude that the God contemplated by our founders, was an agent of the devil. The God we know is busy saving souls, not condemning them to hell.

The unfortunate implication of Justice Holmes' statement is that an American citizen is at liberty to do anything, even to engage in such conduct as may condemn him to hell. Implicit in Holmes' views is the constitutional notion that the Constitution does not embody any particular conception of the good. The logical extension of that notion is that the Constitution itself does not endorse any particular morality. What a secularistic hyperbole! In terms of human rights the Constitution is founded on nothing but morality: of equality among its citizens, of life, liberty and the pursuit of happiness, which are declared endowed by their Creator. As Justice Fields asserted in the 1873 ***Slaughterhouse*** case, speaking to the Fourteenth Amendment:

> "That amendment was intended to give practical effect to the declaration of 1776 of unalienable rights, **rights which are the gift of the Creator; which the law does not confer but only recognizes**."

The interests of secularism and the interests of our Creator are at war with each other and are mutually exclusive. Secularism, as defined by Webster's Dictionary is "a system of doctrines and practices that disregards or rejects any form of religious faith and worship." But our Constitution recognizes that the unalienable rights of we the people are **"rights which are the gift of the Creator"**. Admittedly there are many persons with some learning who are embarrassed to talk about God. But as long as God resides in the very center of our concept of humanity, judges have the inescapable duty to speak of Him who made a gift of unalienable rights to the people of America. Therefore, in terms of human rights and dignity the court is without jurisdictional authority to read God out of the Constitution.

A record of Justice Holmes' liberalism is reflected in his dissent from the decision of the majority in the case of ***Abrams, et al v. United States*** (1919).[33] This case involved the constitutionality of the Espionage Act of Congress. Among the charges filed against the defendants in that case, based on the Espionage Act, was that the defendants conspired "when the United States was at war with the Imperial German Government," and "unlawfully and willfully, by utterance, writing, printing, and publication to urge, incite and advocate curtailment of production of things and products, to-wit, ordnance and ammunition, necessary and essential to the prosecution of the war". Among the speech employed in the publication were:

> "'His [the President's] shameful, cowardly silence about the intervention in Russia reveals the hypocrisy of the plutocratic gang in Washington and vicinity.'
>
> 'He [the President] is too much of a coward to come out openly and say: 'We capitalistic nations cannot afford to have a proletarian republic in Russia.'
>
> "Among the capitalistic nations which the defendant testified the United States was included."

Growing more inflammatory the circular culminates in:

> "'The Russian Revolution cries: 'Workers of the world! Awake! Rise! Put down your enemy and mine!'"
>
> 'Yes friends, there is only one enemy of the workers of the world and that is CAPITALISM.'"

The circular concludes:

> "'Awake! Awake, you Workers of the World!'
>
> REVOLUTIONISTS"

The court concluded that:

> "This is clearly an appeal to the 'workers' of this country to arise and put down by force the government of the

> United States which they characterize as their 'hypocritical,' 'cowardly' and 'capitalistic' enemy."

In referring to another circular the court observed that in referring to "his Majesty, Mr. Wilson, and the rest of the gang, dogs of all colors!" it continued:

> "'Workers, Russian emigrants, you who had the least belief in the honesty of our government,'"

After admitting that the circular had reference to the United States Government, the defendants further asserted:

> "'must now throw away all confidence, must spit in the face the false, hypocritic, military propaganda which has fooled you so relentlessly, calling forth your sympathy, your help, to the prosecution of the war.'"

It goes on:

> "'With the money which you have loaned, or are going to loan them, they will make bullets not only for the Germans, but also for the Workers Soviets of Russia. *Workers in the ammunition factories, you are producing bullets, bayonets, cannon, to murder not only the Germans, but also your dearest, best, who are in Russia and are fighting for freedom.*'"

The majority of the court concluded that:

> "Even if their primary purpose and intent was to aid the cause of the Russian Revolution, the plan of action which

> they adopted necessarily involved, before it could be realized, defeat of the war program of the United States, for the obvious effect of this appeal, if it should become effective, as they hoped it might, would be to persuade persons of character such as those whom they regarded themselves as addressing, not to aid government loans and not to work in ammunition factories, where their work would produce 'bullets, bayonets, cannon' and other munitions of war, the use of which would cause the 'murder' of Germans and Russians."

Quoting further from the circular the court noted the following language by defendants:

> "'America and her Allies have betrayed [the Workers]. Their robberish aims are clear to all men. The destruction of the Russian Revolution, that is the politics of the march to Russia.
>
> *'Workers, our reply to the barbaric intervention has to be a general strike! An open challenge* only will let the government know that not only the Russian Worker fights for *freedom, but also *here in America lives the spirit of Revolution.'*
>
> . . .
>
> 'Do not let the government scare you with their wild punishment in prisons, hanging and shooting. We must not and will not betray the splendid fighters of Russia. *Work-*

> *ers, up to fight.*'"

The court quoted further from the circular demonstrating that the purpose of the speech was to throw the country in a state of revolution, "if possible, and to thereby frustrate the military program of the government." This quote reads:

> "'We, the toilers of America, who believe in real liberty, shall *pledge ourselves*, in case the United States will participate in that bloody conspiracy against Russia, *to create so great a disturbance that the autocrats of America shall be compelled to keep their armies at home, and not be able to spare any for Russia.*'"
>
> . . .
>
> "'If they will use arms against the Russian people to enforce their standard of order, *so will we use arms,* and they shall never see the ruin of the Russian Revolution.'"

A majority of the court concluded that the defendants were guilty as charged and that the freedom of speech guaranteed by the First Amendment could not be interposed as a defense, especially where the action and speech of these defendants sought to overthrow the government and/or materially impair the country's ability to successfully conclude the war in which the country was involved.

Mr. Justice Holmes dissented and Justice Brandeis joined in that dissent. He stated that the government could constitutionally punish speech, but only that speech which:

> "... produces or is intended to produce a clear and imminent danger that it will bring about forthwith certain substantive evils that the United States constitutionally may seek to prevent."

While conceding that there are dangers "peculiar to war, as against others" but he said "the principle of the right to free speech is always the same. It is only the present danger of immediate evil or an intent to bring it about that warrants Congress in setting a limit to the expression of opinion where private rights are not concerned."

Thus Holmes' view was that government could not curtail the individual's right of free speech except when such speech produced "a clear and imminent danger". He does not consider that the pamphlet and speech of these defendants rose to such "a clear and imminent danger". Gifted by superb diction, Holmes made his case in these words:

> "But when men have realized that time has upset many fighting faiths, they may come to believe even more than they believe the very foundations of their own conduct that the ultimate good desired is better reached by free trade in ideas — that the best test of truth is the power of the thought to get itself accepted in the competition of the market, and that truth is the only ground upon which their wishes safely can be carried out. That at any rate is the theory of our Constitution. It is an experiment, as all life is an experiment. Every year if not every day we have to wager our salvation upon some prophecy based upon imperfect knowledge. While that experiment is part of our system I think that we should be eternally vigilant against

> attempts to check the expression of opinions that we loathe and believe to be fraught with death, unless they so imminently threaten immediate interference with the lawful and pressing purposes of the law that an immediate check is required to save the country."

This is classic Holmes and classic "content neutrality". Under the rubric of "truth" Holmes declares that the individual may engage in any type of speech, even advocating the overthrow of government. "Truth", he declared, "is the power of the thought to get itself accepted in the competition of the market". And such a "truth is the <u>only</u> ground upon which their wishes safely can be carried out." Then he says, "that at any rate is the theory of our Constitution".

That is classic sophistry, plausible but constitutionally fallacious. It is based upon the deification of secularism as the god of worship in interpreting the Constitution. It institutionalizes the right of free speech as an absolute right. If, under the auspices of such an absolute right, a citizen may advocate the violent overthrow of our government, the ultimate goal of rebellion, then such absolute right of speech can run amok in the arena of human values such as decency, personal dignity, moral rectitude, self discipline and civic virtue. It unleashes and authorizes a species of speech characterized by intellectual incontinence that is best suited to chaos rather than ordered liberty.

In terms of the personal rights of our citizens our nation is not built on the secularistic notion of truth. Our nation is built upon a religious notion of truth . . . a truth which acknowledges the existence of our Creator. And a Creator of the ultimate truth. Our nation is founded on the fundamental proposition that the rights of our citizens are endowed by our Creator and on that account made unalienable. Advocating sin, moral depravity, profligacy, violence, dishonesty and cruelty falls outside of the unalienable rights of our citizens because these are alien to our founding notion of our Creator.

Now if we the people, where the power of government originates, wish to change our government, we have the power to do so. We the people have the power to amend our Constitution. The means of doing so are peaceful and deliberate. There is no need or room for violent speech or action to accomplish that goal. All that is required is that we cast our vote. So if we want a secularistic deity instead of God as the ultimate guide of our destiny, then we possess the exclusive power to make that choice. And if that choice is made, then Holmes is correct when he says: "Truth is the power of the thought to get itself accepted in the competition of the market". And if that choice is made then Holmes would be correct in saying: "That at any rate is the theory of our Constitution."

Holmes' statement that "time has upset many fighting faiths" is provocative because he implicates free speech among the "faiths" vulnerable to being upset. In assessing such a statement we must never forget that our founders pledged their lives, their property, and sacred honor to the defense of the Declaration of Independence. And we engaged in fighting for that faith more than 200 years ago and won. That faith was enshrined in our written Constitution — a Constitution older than any other the world over. And why is this so? It is because the glue which binds us together in one common purpose is our religiosity, proclaiming a faith in the existence of our Creator as the guiding light of our existence. This is our heritage. This must be our future.

The date is April 25, 1938. The legal virus, randomly traveling the judicial corridors, is beginning now to settle in and play a major role in the decisions of the Supreme Court. ***United States v. Carolene Products Co.***[34] That case involved the power of the national government to regulate interstate commerce. The Carolene Company was shipping in interstate commerce a compound of condensed, skimmed milk and coconut oil made in imitation or semblance of condensed milk or cream. Government indicted this company for violating the "Filled Milk Act" of Congress. The question before the court was whether or not Congress had power to prohibit in interstate commerce skimmed milk compounded with any fat or oil other than milk fat, so as to resemble milk or cream. The court was called upon to determine if the exercise of that power infringed the Fifth Amendment of the defendant, that is the defendant's right to his property without due process of law. In the course of the opinion, the court pointed out that the indictment charges this defendant with placing in interstate commerce "an adulterated article of food injurious to the public health". In its ruling the court stated that Congress

> "is free to exclude from interstate commerce articles whose use in the states for which they are destined it may reasonably conceive to be injurious to the public **health, morals and welfare**."

In speaking to the intrinsic value of the law, the court held that such a legislative act enjoys "**the presumption of constitutionality**". In other words, absent anything overtly unreasonable about such a legislative enactment, the constitutionality of any such legislation is presumed and not open to debate. Furthermore the court held that "the existence of facts supporting the legislative judgment is to be presumed". The court further stated that the decision concerning this statute was for the Congress to make and "neither the finding of a court arrived at by weighing the evidence, nor the verdict of a jury can be substituted for it".

The reader may wonder in reading about this case and ask, "What's new?" True this decision reflects the Jeffersonian approach to the constitutionality of any legislative act which guarantees to the majority their right to embody their opinion, their preferences and decency in legislation as part of the democratic process. So the ***Carolene*** case presented nothing new. What was significant about that decision was not the decision per se, but the footnotes verbalized by Justice Stone who delivered the opinion of the court. In his footnotes, Justice Stone suggested the adoption of a constitutional dichotomy:

> "There may be narrower scope for operation of the presumption of constitutionality when legislation appears on its face to be within a specific prohibition of the Constitution, such as those of the first ten amendments, which are deemed equally specific when held to be embraced within the Fourteenth.
>
> It is unnecessary to consider now whether legislation which restricts those political processes which can ordinarily be expected to bring about repeal of undesirable legislation, is to be subjected to more exacting judicial scrutiny under the general prohibitions of the Fourteenth Amendment than are most other types of legislation."

Justice Stone was effectively saying that when dealing with property interests the "presumption of constitutionality" was less subject to judicial scrutiny. But "more exacting judicial scrutiny" must be exercised by the court when dealing with the "general prohibition of the Fourteenth Amendment". Thus there is proposed a differing standard of review. The differing standards are not based on any special value consideration of any legislation. Instead the judicial review would be in terms of the vulnerability to perversion by laws enacted by the majority. Implicit in that constitutional notion is the directive that limits must be imposed by judicial fiat on permissible democratic purposes, especially when dealing with the liberty interest of the individual. Such a view would engage the judicial branch of government in intruding into the legislative branch of government by limiting the power of the legislative branch to make laws for the good of the majority. This footnote constitutional notion lived long after the opinion of the court faded into oblivion and has continued as the nurturing agency for further restriction on the legislative branch of government and the granting of more liberty rights to the individual, existing on the ruins of the right of the majority to "prevail" in the democratic process. These footnotes were destined to embolden judicial activism as to the application of the Bill of Rights as exemplified by subsequent cases.

What stimulated Stone's novel and esoteric footnotes was the court's earlier decision in ***Palko v. State of Connecticut*** [35] rendered the year before (1937). In the ***Palko*** case the Supreme Court had for review a state statute which gave to the state in criminal cases the right to appeal any verdict rendered against the defendant where the trial court had committed error of law. In the first trial of the defendant he was found guilty of murder in the second degree and sentenced to life imprisonment. The state appealed that verdict, alleging error during the trial. The Supreme Court of Connecticut agreed with the prosecution, reversed the verdict, and remanded the case for new trial. On new trial, ***Palko*** was found guilty of murder and was sentenced to death. The defendant obtained review by the Supreme Court concerning his criminal trial. His contention before court was that by trying him twice the state violated his constitutional right not to be placed in double jeopardy. He argued that the Fifth Amendment, though directed solely to the federal government, which creates immunity from double jeopardy, should be automatically included in the Fourteenth Amendment with the result that the second trial constituted a violation of his immunity from double jeopardy.

Mr. Justice Cardozo wrote the opinion of the court. He conceded that the Fifth Amendment had been held to forbid "jeopardy in the same case if the new trial was at the instance of the government and not upon defendant's motion". That was ***Palko's*** situation. The court however refused to hold that the Fourteenth Amendment absorbed the provisions of the Fifth Amendment. In the process the court, for example, said that while under the Fifth Amendment no person shall be held to answer for a capital crime "unless on presentment or indictment of a grand jury". To the contrary, by an earlier decision the Supreme Court had held that the state could constitutionally initiate such a prosecution by way of a bill of information brought by the prosecutor in such a case. The court selectively gave other examples of the difference between the requirements of the Fifth Amendment and the approved practices of the states under the Fourteenth Amendment. Further Justice Cardozo stated that the right of "immunity from prosecution, except as the result of an indictment, may have value and importance. Even so, they are not of the very essence of the scheme of ordered liberty." They do not represent "a principle of justice so rooted in the traditions and conscience of our people as to be ranked as fundamental". The court observed that the state law of Connecticut simply put the state and the accused on the same level ground, granting to each the right of appeal from any verdict which was the product of error of law. Thus in this case the court only selectively included in the Fourteenth Amendment those notions of justice "so rooted in the traditions and conscience of our people as to be ranked as fundamental" and rejected the total incorporation of the Fifth Amendment into the Fourteenth Amendment. This was soon to change. Such things as "content neutrality" as opposed to what I perceive to be "content engagement", the autonomy of the individual, unencumbered by any of our traditions, values and notions of moral responsibility, were to be elevated as dominant interpretative devices that would release the court of its obligation of assessing the intrinsic value of any law before it and its utility to society as expressed by the majority of we the people.

CHAPTER SEVEN

THE ROCK AND ROLL CONSTITUTIONAL DANCE

In his early days, Justice Holmes was the model of judicial self-restraint and the defender of our three-branch functional structure of government. In his first written opinion as a Justice of the Supreme Court in 1903 in the case of ***Otis & Gassman v. Parker*** [36] Justice Holmes expressed his role as judge. In the ***Otis*** case there was involved the state constitution of California which provided that all contracts "for the sale of shares of the capital stock of any corporation or association, on margin, are to be delivered at a future day, shall be void, and any money paid on such contract may be recovered by the party paying it . . ." The defendant, Parker, was sued based on a claimed violation of this California law. Parker contended that this law infringed his freedom of contract right and was a denial of his property without due process of law. Intermediary courts had affirmed the constitutionality of this California law.

And the Supreme Court, in an opinion by Justice Holmes, affirmed that law as being constitutional. In upholding the state law as constitutional Justice Holmes focused on the interpretation role of the court in giving effect to the majority's conception of the good life. Said Justice Holmes:

> "While the courts must exercise a judgment of their own, it by no means is true that every law is void which may seem to the judges who pass upon it excessive, unsuited to its ostensible end, or based upon conceptions of morality with which they disagree."

What Justice Holmes was saying in 1903 is that legislation either by the states or the national government, must remain undisturbed by the court even though it "may seem" to the judges that the legislation is "excessive, unsuited to its ostensible end, or based upon conceptions of morality with which they [the judges] disagree". He stated that such a deference to the legislative action is necessary in order to allow "for differences of view, as well as for possible peculiar conditions which this court can know but imperfectly, if at all". Then Holmes stated:

> "Otherwise a constitution, instead of embodying only relatively fundamental rules of right, as generally understood by all English-speaking communities, would become the partisan of a particular set of ethical or economical opinions, which by no means are held *semper ubique et ab omnibus.*" (always, everywhere, and from everyone)

Further Holmes said:

> "If the state thinks that an admitted evil cannot be prevented except by prohibiting a calling or transaction not

> in itself necessarily objectionable, the courts cannot interfere, unless, in looking at the substance of the matter, they can see that it 'is a clear, unmistakable infringement of rights secured by the fundamental law.'"

Here Holmes is saying that it is the duty of judges to look at the substantive value of the action sought to be advocated or denied by the law under review. This rule of interpretation can aptly be described as "content engagement" as opposed to "content neutrality". The "content engagement" rule is in harmony with the original intent of our Constitution because that interpretation approach is the only effective way to insure that the right of the majority is to prevail. And such an interpretation is the only reasonable way to maintain a separation of powers expressed in our Constitution. But the longer Holmes stayed on the bench as Judge, the more he moved away from this original formula for the interpretation of the Constitution as shown by his opinions in the ***Truax, Abrams*** and ***Gitlow*** cases, mentioned before.

The move away from the concept of "content engagement" to "content neutrality" was at first subtle and clothed in eloquent prose which masked the underlying, inchoate judicial virulence inimical to the original intent of our founders. To appreciate fully this subtle change we must understand clearly the concept of "content engagement." The concept of "content engagement" is the process in or by which the court is to give effect to our laws and our system of government. This process acknowledges that the national government is a government of delegated powers, powers delegated to it by the several states. And all powers not delegated are reserved to the states. Every law, even those "which may seem to the judges who pass upon it excessive, unsuited to its ostensible end, or based upon conceptions of morality with which they disagree" are not void on that account but on the contrary must be accepted as valid. The courts cannot "interfere" with such laws, unless, "in looking at the substance of the matter," judges can see that such laws are "a clear, unmistakable infringement of rights secured by the fundamental law." And as stated by Justice Cardozo in ***Polko*** laws are "fundamental" which are "rooted in the traditions and conscience of our people." This process of "content engagement," therefore, imposes upon the courts an institutional deference to legislative action in order to allow "for differences of view, as well as for possible peculiar conditions", which the Supreme Court "can know but imperfectly, if at all." Otherwise, as Justice Holmes stated, our constitution "would become the partisan of a particular set of ethical or economical opinions" which by no means are held always, everywhere, and by everyone. That in any case is the rule of law of our constitution as originally conceived by the founders of our nation. Analytical scrutiny of significant Supreme Court decisions regarding principles of freedom of religion, freedom of speech and freedom of privacy instances unwarranted assaults upon and disingenuous circumventions of our institutional protocol of government and principles of justice.

CHAPTER EIGHT

FREEDOM OF RELIGION

In part pertinent the First Amendment reads:

"Congress shall make no law respecting an establishment of religion or prohibiting the free exercise thereof."

The first notable case involving the interpretation of freedom of religion occurred in 1878 in the case of ***Reynolds v. United States***. [37] Reynolds was charged with the crime of bigamy prohibited by federal law. Reynolds was a member of the Church of Jesus Christ of Latter Day Saints, commonly called the Mormon Church and as such a believer in the religious doctrine of polygamy. He was tried and convicted under the statute. On appeal he contended that his religious belief must be accepted as a justification for the violation of the criminal statute. The Supreme Court affirmed his conviction. In affirming Reynolds' conviction the court held that the free exercise clause of the first amendment protected religious beliefs, and not necessarily religious practices. In speaking to religious beliefs the court enlisted Jefferson's conception of religion. Jefferson, said the court, stated that "religion is a matter which lies solely between man and his God" and that man accounts "to none other for his faith or his worship" but to God. And because of this "the legislative powers of the government reach actions only, and not opinions." The court, therefore, concluded that one's religious belief is beyond the control of government and protected by the free exercise clause of the First Amendment.

Religious practice, on the other hand, was a different matter. The free exercise clause of the First Amendment did not protect all religious practices. But as to such practices the government had the power to control or prohibit those thought to be offensive to society. After engaging in a brief review of religious history, the court concluded that polygamy was not an accepted practice. In support of that conclusion the court stated, "polygamy has always been odious among the northern and western nations of Europe and, until the establishment of the Mormon Church, was almost exclusively a feature of the life of Asiatic and African people."

To permit such a practice, said the court:

> "would be to make the professed doctrines of religious belief superior to the law of the land, and in effect to permit every citizen to become a law unto himself."

Thus the court concluded that religious belief was impervious to government interference, but religious practice was subject to government control. This constitutional principle was again to be affirmed as late as 1990.

Originally the First Amendment, like the first ten amendments, applied only against the national government. In 1940, however, the Supreme Court in the case of ***Cantwell, et al v. Connecticut*** [38] ruled that it was incorporated in or absorbed by the Fourteenth Amendment. That decision is significant for more than that reason. The court spoke to the tension between the right of the individual to communicate to others his religious beliefs and the authority of government to maintain public peace and order.

Defendants, members of a group known as Jehovah's Witnesses, decided that they would go out in search of converts; they would go house to house and stop persons on the public streets and try to proselytize or persuade them to their religious beliefs. They armed themselves with religious pamphlets and a victrola recording, which spoke to their beliefs. On that day, they accosted two individuals, who were Catholic in a highly Catholic community, and secured their permission to play the recording which they had and to give them some of their pamphlets. The court describes the encounter between defendants and the individuals on the public streets in Connecticut as follows:

> "The record played by Cantwell embodies a general attack on all organized religious systems as instruments of Satan and injurious to man; it then singles out the Roman Catholic Church for strictures couched in terms which naturally would offend not only persons of that persuasion, but all others who respect the honestly held religious faith of their fellows. The hearers were in <u>fact highly offended</u>. One of them said he felt like <u>hitting Cantwell</u> and the other that he was tempted to <u>throw Cantwell off</u>

> the street. The one who testified he felt like hitting Cantwell said, in answer to the question 'Did you do anything else or have any other reaction?' 'No, sir, because he said he would take the victrola and he went.' The other witness testified that he told Cantwell he had better get off the street before something happened to him and that was the end of the matter as Cantwell picked up his books and walked up the street."

The State argued that such speech and conduct on the public streets violated its law against incitement to breach of the peace and good order, for which defendant should be punished. The court agreed that even the right of free speech or the free exercise of religious practices guaranteed by the First Amendment was subject to control by state law. Here are the words of the court:

> "No one would have the hardihood to suggest that the principle of freedom of speech sanctions incitement to riot or that religious liberty connotes the privilege to exhort others to physical attack upon those belonging to another sect. When clear and present danger of riot, disorder, interference with traffic upon the public streets, or other immediate threat to public safety, peace, or order, appears, the power of the state to prevent or punish is obvious."

But, said the court, "equally obvious is it that a state may not unduly suppress free communication of views, religious or other, under the guise of conserving desirable conditions." The court then concluded the defendants' conduct did not create a "clear and present danger" to peace or to the disturbance of good order. This conclusion was maintained, even though the court admitted that to persuade others the pleader at times "resorts to exaggeration, to vilification of men who have been, or are, prominent in church or state, and even to false statement." The court then reversed the conviction of these defendants.

Two interesting questions of law regarding freedom of speech and freedom of religion are presented by this decision. The first question presented is what does and what does not constitute "incitement to the disturbance of peace or good order" or stated otherwise what constitutes a "clear and present danger" to good order. Is "clear and present danger" an abstract concept malleable to accommodate the predilections or preferences of the judge, or does it exemplify an objective physical fact which speaks for itself? As the court admits, one of the individuals accosted "felt like hitting Cantwell." The other testified that he told Cantwell he "had better get off the street before something happened to him." Thus undeniably the defendants' speech and religious persuasion made these two witnesses feel like punching Cantwell. If, therefore, the "clear and present danger" rule is an abstract concept, or state of mind then it existed as a fact. The danger of a disturbance was avoided not by the nature of the speech but by the fact that Cantwell hit the road. On the other hand, if the "clear and present danger" of inciting a disturbance is exemplified by an objective physical fact, i.e., an actual physical act then there did not exist a "clear and present danger" because it did not materialize into a physical fact. It is apparent, at least in this case, that the "clear and present danger" rule is not a sufficiently reliable test by which the constitutional right of free of speech and freedom of religion is to be determined.

Another interesting legal question presented by this decision regarding the free exercise of religion relates to the fact that the speech and conduct involved occurred on a public street maintained and financed by the state of Connecticut. That question implicates the separation of state and church law, and particularly the establishment clause of the First Amendment. The fact of the matter is that the state of Connecticut indirectly sponsored the religious speech of the defendants by permitting such conduct and speech to take place on public property owned and/or maintained and financially supported by it. Because no mention was ever made of such an argument, it must be because it occurred to no one that such a fact is a reliable basis to conclude that the state was engaged in the establishment or sponsorship of a particular religion. What makes this legal question so fascinating is the fact that, as we shall see in later decisions, the right to teach religion or pray in public schools was denied based exclusively on the fact that the state or political entity involved maintained and/or financially supported the school facilities.

In 1947 the court was presented with a religion oriented law where the First Amendment was implicated, ***Everson, et al v. Board of Education of Ewing Tp***[39] The essential facts in the case were that the New Jersey law involved authorized reimbursement to parents of money expended by them for the transportation of their children on regular buses operated by the public transportation system. Part of this money was for the payment of transportation of some children in the community to Catholic schools. Everson challenged the right of the state agency to make such reimbursement, claiming that his tax money was being used to support a religion not of his own choosing and, therefore, the law violated the First Amendment. Justice Black wrote the opinion and, in order to place the constitutional question in context, he commented on the history of religion during the days of the settlers and during the days of the old world. He stated that a large proportion of the early settlers of America came here from Europe to escape bondage from laws which compelled them to support and attend government favored churches. And, said Justice Black, "centuries immediately before and contemporaneous with the colonization of America had been filled with turmoil, civil strife, and persecutions, generated in large part by established sects to maintain their absolute political and religious supremacy". In that context said Black:

> "Catholics found themselves hounded and proscribed because of their faith; Quakers who followed their conscience went to jail; Baptists were peculiarly obnoxious to certain dominant Protestant sects; men and women of varied faiths who happened to be in a minority in a particular locality were persecuted because they steadfastly persisted in worshiping God only as their own consciences dictated."

Black then referred to Thomas Jefferson, author of the proposed "Virginia Bill of Religious Liberty". In the preamble Jefferson declared:

> "Almighty God hath created the mind free; that all attempts to influence it by temporal punishments, or burthens, or by civil incapacitations, tend only to beget habits of hypocrisy and meanness, and are a departure from the plan of the Holy author of our religion . . ."

Justice Black then adopted Jefferson's view that "the clause against establishment of religion by law was intended to erect a 'wall of separation between Church and State.'" He defined the establishment of religion clause of the First Amendment in these words:

> "The 'establishment of religion' clause of the First Amendment means at least this: Neither a state nor the Federal Government can set up a church. Neither can pass laws which aid one religion, aid all religions, or prefer one religion over another. Neither can force nor influence a person to go to or to remain away from church against his will or force him to profess a belief or disbelief in any religion. No person can be punished for entertaining or professing religious beliefs or disbeliefs, for church attendance or non-attendance. No tax in any amount, large or small, can be levied to support any religious activities or institutions, whatever they may be called, or whatever form they may adopt to teach or practice religion."

Justice Black further spoke to the effect of this establishment clause as follows:

> "That amendment requires the state to be a neutral in its relations with groups of religious believers and non-believers."

The court concluded that the law in controversy was one of general application. And because it was such a law, the Catholics and other religious sects and private schools received state financial help as an incident of citizenship and not as an incident of any religious affiliation. The court then ruled that this state law did not violate the First Amendment right of freedom of religion. This is the all or nothing rule of law which applies to religious freedom under the First Amendment.

Two legal postulates of historic significance should be noted. First, that the First Amendment "required the state to be NEUTRAL, in its relations with groups of religious believers and non-believers".

And second, it is significant because in later cases the court has extrapolated this neutrality rule and made it applicable to individual's rights under other amendments, where their text did not express or imply such neutrality. And in such cases, in the process of fulfilling this concept of neutrality the court abdicated its duty to look at the substantive value of the action sought to be advocated or denied. If the court had not abdicated this duty in later cases, but on the contrary, had performed that duty of interpretation, it would have been compelled to be loyal to the legal principle that a law must remain undisturbed by the court even though it "may seem" to the judges that the legislation is "excessive, unsuited to its ostensible end or based upon conceptions of morality with which they [the judges] disagree", as stated by Justice Holmes in the ***Otis*** case earlier mentioned. Thus the conception of the good of our society as ordained by the majority was soon to become off-limits for the Supreme Court because of the court's self-imposed neutrality.

POST MORTEM. This ruling of the court, if still effective, would give legitimacy to vouchers that might be given to parents who choose to have their children enroll in other than public schools. This is especially true since the offer of vouchers are made generally to all parents as an incident of citizenship and not as an incident of religious affiliations.

This decision was followed in 1961by the case of ***People of State of Illinois ex rel. McCollum v. Board of Education, et al*** .[40] In that case the School Board allowed the use of the school building for the teaching of religion by a group composed of Jewish, Roman Catholic and Protestant faiths. Such teaching took place weekly for thirty minutes for the lower grades, forty-five minutes for the higher. The attendance of a pupil in the teaching of religion is consensual. Both the student and the parents of the students consented to such religion instructions. No student was compelled against his will to receive such instruction. Those consenting were released temporarily from their regular school classes for the limited purpose of attending the religious classes. Justice Black wrote the majority opinion. In the process he rationalized that the "utilization of the tax established and tax supported public school system to aid religious groups to spread their faith," violated the First Amendment. He then revisited the ***Everson*** case where the court had held:

> "Neither a state nor the Federal Government can set up a church. Neither can pass laws which aid one religion, aid all religions, or prefer one religion over another . . .."

In justification of that sweeping proscription Justice Black asserted:

> "For the First Amendment rests upon the premise that both religion and government can best work to achieve their lofty aims if each is left free from the other within its respective sphere. Or, as we said in the Everson case, the First amendment has erected a wall between Church and State which must be kept high and impregnable."

Justice Reed entered a vigorous dissent. Essentially his dissent was predicated on the historic relationship of State and Church. In his critical analysis of the majority opinion Justice Reed observed that the majority never concluded that the religious teachings involved constituted "an establishment of religion", nor an interference with the exercise of religion. Justice Reed referred to the majority opinion in its reference to Jefferson's statement of the "wall of separation". In so doing he made reference to Jefferson's view of the relationship between State and Church as recorded on October 7, 1822 in his capacity as Rector to the President's Directors of the Literary Fund. He quoted the following statement made by Jefferson:

> "Should the religious sects of this State, or any of them, according to the invitation held out to them, establish within, or adjacent to, the precincts of the University, schools for instruction in the religion of their sect, the students of the University will be free, and expected to attend religious worship at the establishment of their respective sects, in the morning, and in times to meet their school in the University at its stated hour."

Further, Justice Reed concluded that the "wall of separation between church and state" that Mr. Jefferson built at the university which he founded did not exclude religious education from that school. Further Justice Reed observed:

> "The difference between the generality of his statements on the separation of church and state and the specificity of his conclusions on education are considerable. A rule of law should not be drawn from a figure of speech."

Further Reed stated "this court cannot be too cautious in upsetting practices embedded in our society by many years of experience".

And finally Justice Reed concluded:

> "Devotion to the great principle of religious liberty should

> not lead us into a rigid interpretation of the constitutional guarantee that conflicts with accepted habits of our people. This is an instance where, for me, the history of past practices is determinative of the meaning of a constitutional clause not a decorous introduction to the study of its text."

Ironically it was okay in 1940, as in the ***Cantwell*** case, to teach and preach religion on "tax supported and tax established" public streets. But by 1961 such religious activities on "tax established and tax supported public school" was unconstitutional. And thus the constitutional dance goes on.

In 1961 the Supreme Court had for consideration the validity of the Sunday Closing Law enacted by the state of Pennsylvania, ***Braunfeld v. Brown*** [41] The attack on the constitutionality of Philaldelphia's Sunday Closing Law was made by Jewish merchants who were members of the Orthodox Jewish faith. Merchandise which they sold fell within the proscription of the Pennsylvania law. Their legal position before the court was that the religious Sabbath of the Jewish faith required these merchants to close on Saturday and not Sunday. During their Sabbath day, their competitors conducted business as usual. In essence these merchants contended that the result of the law under consideration compelled them to give up their Sabbath observance, a basic tenet of the Orthodox Jewish faith, or suffer serious economic disadvantage should they continue to adhere to their Sabbath. Corollary to the argument was that Sunday was the Sabbath for religions other than the Sabbath of Orthodox Jewish faith; therefore, the state law favored these religions over the Jewish Sabbath. The court held that the Pennsylvania statute did not violate these merchants' First Amendment right of religious freedom.

In rationalizing its opinion the court observed that "the freedom to hold religious beliefs and opinions is absolute". In support of that statement the court referred to the earlier ***Barnette*** decision, extrapolating from that decision that no law is constitutional which compels students to salute a flag, where the students' religious belief prohibits flag saluting. A reference then was made to Thomas Jefferson and his express view concerning religion. Quoting Jefferson:

> "Believing with you that religion is a matter which lies solely between man and his God, that he owes account to none other for his faith or his worship, that the *legislative powers of government reach actions only and not opinions*, I contemplate with sovereign reverence that act of the whole American people which declared that their legislature should 'make no law respecting an establishment of religion, or prohibiting the free exercise thereof,' thus building a wall of separation between church and State."

The court concluded that the Pennsylvania statute neither outlawed, criminalized, nor interfered with the religious practice of the Orthodox Jews. It concluded that Sunday was a secular day of rest, the religious protestations to the contrary notwithstanding; Sunday was:

> "One day of the week apart from the others as a day of rest, repose, recreation and tranquility—a day when the hectic tempo of every day existence ceases and a more pleasant atmosphere is created, a day which all members of the family and community have the opportunity to spend and enjoy together, a day on which people may visit friends and relatives who are not available during working days,

a day when the weekly laborer may best regenerate himself."

Thus the court concluded that a Sabbath day to one is a recreational day to another. Concluding that the state law in question did not affect the religious beliefs of the Jewish merchants and that it was a law falling within the power of the state to enact, the court denied all relief and held the state law constitutional.

Two years later in ***Sherbert v. Verner*** [42], the court was again confronted with the contention between the religious scruples of the individual and the authority of the state. Sherbert was a member of the Seventh-day Adventist Church and was discharged by her South Carolina employer because she would not work on Saturday, the Sabbath day of her faith. When she was unable to obtain other employment because she would not take Saturday work, she filed a claim for unemployment compensation benefits with the state. The Unemployment Compensation Law provided that to be eligible for benefits, the claimant must be "able to work and *** is available for work". Such a claimant is "ineligible for benefits" where he has failed without good cause "to accept available, suitable work when offered him by the employment office or the employer". She was unable to gain employment because she refused to work on Saturday. She contended that the state statute abridged her right to the free exercise of her religion secured under the "Free Exercise Clause" of the First Amendment through the Fourteenth Amendment. Justice Brennan, speaking for the majority, ruled that the state law imposed a burden on the free exercise of her religion; that her "declared ineligibility for benefits derived solely from the practice of her religion", leaving her with the options or choice of foregoing her religious scruples for employment or foregoing employment for her religious scruples. And that, accordingly, the state law was unconstitutional.

It is to be noted that the difference between the 1961 ***Braunfeld*** decision and this decision is the difference between twiddle dee and twiddle da. Such a view is persuasively stated by dissenting Justice Harlan. In his dissent Justice Harlan said:

> "What the Court is holding is that if the State chooses to condition unemployment compensation on the applicant's availability for work, it is constitutionally compelled to *carve out an exception* — and to provide benefits — for those whose unavailability is due to their religious convictions."

He pointed out that this decision overruled ***Braunfeld v. Brown*** which held that it did not offend the "free exercise" clause of the constitution "for a state to forbid a Sabbatarian to do business on Sunday". Further he emphasized that the "secular purpose of the statute before us today is even clearer than that involved in ***Braunfeld***". Justice Harlan concluded by observing that the state could tailor its legislation in such a manner as to avoid such a controversy. And he complained that the "neutrality" rule in religious matters "is not so narrow a channel that the slightest deviation from an absolutely straight course leads to condemnation". Then he concluded:

> "Such compulsion in the present case is particularly inappropriate in light of the indirect, remote and insubstantial effect of the decision below on the exercise of appellant's religion and in light of the direct financial assistance to the religion that today's decision requires."

And so goes the rock and roll constitutional dance.

The next notable case involving the free exercise clause of the First Amendment occurred in 1968 in ***Epperson v. Arkansas*** [43]. That case involved the constitutionality of an Arkansas statute that prohibited the teaching of Darwin's Theory of Evolution. This theory is commonly referred to as the "monkey law". The state law prohibited the teaching of the Darwin theory that mankind "descended from a lower order of animals". Susan Epperson, a young woman who graduated from Arkansas' school system and then obtained a master's degree in zoology at the University of Illinois, was employed by the Little Rock school system to teach tenth grade biology at Central High School. In embarking upon her teaching she was troubled by the existence of the state statute that made it a crime to teach Darwin's Theory of Evolution. Her concern arose from the fact that one of the biology textbooks devoted a chapter to that theory. She sought judicial relief by filing a lawsuit in an Arkansas state court seeking to have the statute declared unconstitutional. Eventually in 1968 her case was presented to the Supreme Court. The Supreme Court declared the statute unconstitutional as being in violation of the free exercise clause of the First Amendment and offered the following rationale:

> "The overriding fact is that Arkansas' law selects from the body of knowledge a particular segment which it proscribes for the sole reason that it is deemed to conflict with a particular religious doctrine; that is, with a particular interpretation of the Book of Genesis by a particular religious group."

Justice Black reluctantly concurred with the opinion primarily because it was burdened with a doubtful statement of the law applicable. For example, he posed the question:

> "If the theory is considered anti-religious, as the Court indicates, how can the State be bound by the Federal Constitution to permit its teachers to advocate such an "anti-religious"doctrine to schoolchildren?"

In other words Justice Black, building upon the free exercise clause of the First Amendment, which prohibits any state to enact any legislation which "aid or oppose" any religion, declared that by compelling the teaching of Darwin's Theory of Evolution, the court was sustaining a state statute which "opposed" a religion, which itself is constitutionally prohibited. He made the further observation that the removal of the subject of evolution would leave the state in a "neutral" position towards these "supposedly competing religious and anti-religious doctrines". Unlike previous cases, neutrality was unceremoniously not invited to participate in this opinion.

In 1984 a crack in the wall of separation between Church and State occurred, and through that crack shown a brilliant ray of hope for the accommodation of religion as an historic, viable component of our nation's character and destiny. The harbinger of that event was the case of ***Lynch v. Donnelly*** [44], which stemmed the red tide of secularism as the alternative to our God-oriented philosophy of government. The essential facts of that case involved the action of the city of Pawtucket, R.I., in annually erecting a Christmas display in a park owned by a nonprofit organization located in the heart of the city shopping district. The display included, in addition to such objects as a Santa Claus house, a Christmas tree, and a banner that read "SEASONS GREETINGS," a creche or

Nativity scene which had been part of the annual display for 40 years or more. The A.C.L.U. joined with certain residents of Pawtucket and filed a lawsuit seeking to enjoin the city from sponsoring this Christmas display, claiming that this was a violation of the separation clause of the First Amendment. The Supreme Court on review held that there was no violation of the separation clause and dismissed the lawsuit. At the very outset Justice Burger, speaking for the majority, explained that the purpose of the First Amendment regarding religion was:

> "To prevent, as far as possible, the intrusion of either [the church or the state] into the precincts of the other."

But Justice Burger postulated the *caveat*:

> "Total separation is not possible in an absolute sense. Some relationship between government and religious organizations is inevitable."

Justice Burger adverted to the metaphorical statement attributed to Jefferson to the effect that there was a wall of separation between the state and religion, and said:

> "The metaphor has served as a reminder that the Establishment Clause forbids an established church or anything approaching it. But the metaphor itself is not a wholly accurate description of the practical aspects of the relationship that in fact exists between church and state.
>
> No significant segment of our society and no institution within it can exist in a vacuum or in total or absolute isolation from all the other parts, much less from govern-

> ment. * * *
>
> Nor does the Constitution require complete separation of church and state; it affirmatively mandates accommodation, not merely tolerance, of all religions, and forbids hostility toward any."

Justice Burger reached back into history and asserted that at the first session of the First Congress in 1789, at a time when the First Amendment was approved, "it enacted legislation providing for paid Chaplains for the House and Senate." He further noted that members of the First Congress had been delegates to the Constitutional Convention where freedom of speech, press and religion were the subjects of frequent discussions. He posited that these delegates saw "no conflict with the Establishment Clause when Nebraska employed members of the clergy as official legislative Chaplains to give opening prayers at sessions of the state legislature." The Congress of 1789 voiced no establishment problem in the employment of congressional Chaplains to offer daily prayers in the Congress, "a practice that has continued for nearly two centuries". It was the original intention of the founders of America, said Justice Burger, to accommodate religious beliefs. He emphasized that there was an unbroken history of official acknowledgment by all three branches of government of the role of religion in American life. Burger then quoted an earlier statement by former Justice Douglas:

> "We are a religious people whose institutions presuppose a Supreme Being."

He pointed out that in the early colonial period a day of Thanksgiving was celebrated as a religious holiday "to give thanks for the bounties of Nature as gifts from God." In fact, he emphasized President Washington and his successors proclaimed Thanksgiving "with all of its religious overtones", a day of national celebration. Christmas was likewise proclaimed as a national holiday. Chaplains of the Senate, the House and the military receive compensation from government for their religious services. He pointed out that other examples of "our religious heritage" are found in the statutorily prescribed national motto "In God We Trust", which Congress and the President mandated for our currency and in our Pledge of Allegiance language which identifies a religious character of our nation in these words: "One nation under God". He further pointed out that the National Gallery in Washington, "maintained with government support" has long exhibited "masterpieces with religious messages", among which is the "Last Supper, and paintings depicting the Birth of Christ, the Crucifixion, and the Resurrection". Then he referred to the chamber of the Supreme Court saying it was decorated with a notable and permanent symbol of religion: "Moses with the Ten Commandments". He observed that Congress directed the President to proclaim a National Day of Prayer each year "on which [day] the people of the United States may turn to God in prayer and meditation at churches, in groups, and as individuals". Presidential proclamations have also issued to commemorate "Jewish Heritage Week and Jewish High Holy Days". Justice Burger further ruled that "the display engenders a friendly community spirit of good will in keeping with the season". The display thus serves a secular purpose. "And the fact that the creche" may have special meaning to some religious faithful, it does not follow that the practice or the law involved interferes with the establishment or practice of religion. Finally Justice Burger said:

> "It would be ironic, however, if the inclusion of a single symbol of a particular historic religious event, as part of a celebration acknowledged in the Western World for 20 centuries, an in this country by the people, by the Executive Branch, by the Congress, and the courts for 2 centuries, would so "taint" the City's exhibit as to render it violative of the Establishment Clause. To forbid the use of this one passive symbol—the creche—at the very time people are taking note of the season with Christmas hymns and carols in public schools and other public places, and while the Congress and legislatures open sessions with prayers by paid chaplains, would be a stilted overreaction contrary to our history and to our holdings."

Justice Brennen recorded a stinging dissent in this case. To understand his remarks it is helpful to recall his view as to the separation of state and religion. It was in the McCollum case that he contended that government, in the pursuit of its secularistic mission, and religion, in the pursuit of its spiritual mission, can "best work to achieve their lofty aims if each is left free from the other within its respective's sphere."

In his dissent Justice Brennen rebuked the majority for trivializing the legal test earlier postulated by the court in determining whether any law or action violates the separation of church and state rule of the First Amendment. This test is known as the Lemon test, asserted in the case of ***Lemon v. Kurtzman***, in 1971. This is a three-prong test:

> "First, the [practice] must have a secular legislative purpose; second, its principal or primary effect must be one that neither advances nor inhibits religion; finally, [it] must

> not foster an excessive government entanglement with religion."

Brennen argued that the creche "is the chief symbol of the characteristically Christian belief that a divine Savior was brought into the world and that the purpose of this miraculous birth was to illuminate a path towards salvation and redemption for Christians, that path is exclusive, precious, and holy." He then asserted that the "primary effect" of including this nativity scene in the City's display is "to place the government's imprimatur of approval on the particular religious beliefs exemplified by the creche." In effect, therefore, Brennen asserted the approval by the City of the creche in the display intended to officially advance the Christian religion in violation of the establishment clause of the First Amendment. He also reminded Christians that they had achieved a pyrrhic victory in this case, that is, the price they paid far outweighed the victory they achieved. This was especially true, he contended, because the profound symbol of the creche was characterized as but a secularistic traditional symbol. Witness his inimitable words:

> "To suggest, as the Court does, that such a symbol is merely 'traditional' and therefore no different from Santa's house or reindeer is not only offensive to those for whom the creche has profound significance, but insulting to those who insist for religious or personal reasons that the story of Christ is in no sense a part of 'history' nor an unavoidable element of our national 'heritage.'"

This case more classically than others represents the pros and cons of the separation of State and Church. Many responsible religious commentators protest bitterly against the commercialization of Christmas as a debasement of the spiritual nature and meaning of Christianity. Yet, for the most part, Christians universally approve of the public display of the creche in government sponsored displays. Such an ambivalence is not easily reconcilable, if at all. The court rationalizes and, therefore, allows government to sponsor a public display of the creche by characterizing the creche as but a secular notion of a public celebration. Yet, second only to the cross, the creche is the most profound symbol of Christian faith and belief. Is the Christian's need to spread the faith so great that he is willing to accept a religious profanity? Seemingly so. But such a willingness is neither new nor surprising to Christianity. Apostle Paul felt that way. In addressing the Corinthians he proclaims: "I have become all things to all men so that by all possible means I might save some. I do all this for the sake of the gospel, that I may share in its blessings."

The carving of a niche for religion in government is neither easy to rationalize nor satisfactory to exclude. The decision of the court was divided by five justices for and four against. But as Justice Douglas said:

> "We are a religious people whose institutions presuppose
> a Supreme Being."

And our religiosity is the glue that holds us together in an amalgam of purpose and destiny. It is the spirit of our nation and the comfort of our people.

CHAPTER NINE

FREEDOM OF SPEECH

In part pertinent, the First Amendment to our Constitution provides:

> "Congress shall make no law . . . abridging the Freedom of Speech, or of the press.."

We start this march of inquiry with the postulate that no freedom guaranteed by the several amendments to our constitution is absolute, except freedom of religious belief. This absolute rule regarding the non-absolute nature of our constitutional freedom rights gave rise to a judicial playground for the swing and sway of constitutional interpretation. At stake throughout this process has been the concept of human dignity, its promotion and protection within the parameters of our philosophy of government and justice, a government conceived and committed to the existence of a Supreme Being. From the beginning of our nation we have empowered nine individuals, functioning as justices of our Supreme Court, as the final arbiters of who we are as a nation and what are our fundamental rights and duties as citizens of that nation. These justices are appointed by the President, with the consent of the Senate, for life, removable only by impeachment or death. By nature the power conferred is awesome, the trust imparted is inviolate. Where we come from and where we are headed, and how we traveled along the way, therefore, are exemplified by notable decisions of the Supreme Court.

On March 9, 1942, three months after the beginning of World War II, the court was called upon to decide the range of free speech guaranteed by the First Amendment in the case of ***Chaplinsky v. State of New Hampshire.*** [45] In this case one ***Chaplinsky***, a Jehovah's Witness, was charged with violating a New Hampshire statute prohibiting the addressing of any offensive, derisive or annoying word to any other person who is lawfully in any street or other public place, or calling him by any offensive or derisive name. ***Chaplinsky***, while on a public street near City Hall addressed to another citizen "you are a God damned racketeer and a damned fascist and the whole government of Rochester are fascists . . ." He was convicted of violating this state law and on appeal to the Supreme Court contended that this statute constituted an "unreasonable restraint of Freedom of Speech." The Supreme Court agreed with the state court and affirmed ***Chaplinsky's*** conviction. In doing so, the court stated:

> "It is well understood that the right of free speech is not absolute at all times and under all circumstance. There are certain well-defined and narrowly limited classes of speech, the . . . punishment of which has never been

> thought to raise any Constitutional problem. These include the lewd and obscene, the profane, libelous, and the insulting or 'fighting' words - - those which by their very utterance inflict injury or tend to incite an immediate breach of the peace."

The court then engaged in placing a value on this speech, saying that such speech do not form any essential part "of any exposition of ideas, and are of such slight social value as a step to truth that any benefit that may be derived from them is clearly outweighed by the social interest in order and morality." In other words, the court placed constitutional speech in a high value/low value scale to determine its value to society. The speech in question was considered to be low value in that it did not form an essential part of exposing ideas and was of "slight social value" as a step "to truth" as to be "clearly outweighed by the social interest in order and morality." Thus, as of 1942, the value of constitutional speech was tested against the interest of society to peace and good order and to morality, and such speech was found to be inferior to such societal interests and therefore was not constitutionally protected by the First Amendment of free speech.

Grave social unrest over the plight of the negro race (African Americans) gripped America in the wake of World War II, in such a manner as to shape a species of judicial activism never before witnessed in the judicial history of America. During the war young black Americans in the armed forces were exposed to a new and unimaginable social environment while serving in Europe. They were accepted by European white males and females on a social level comparable to white Americans. It was an experience they probably dreamed of but never realized or expected while living in America. But during the war they fought for freedom and they tasted freedom and it felt good. On their return to America after the war, they allowed themselves to believe that such freedom was achievable in America. It was a dream they thought could possibly come true. They were not alone in such a belief. Their place in American history was under intense scrutiny at that time. In political terms the negro was an invisible man. As one historian put it,

> "America was living a lie for most of the twentieth century. The ideals that were supposed to define the nation were betrayed every hour, every day, for the one-tenth of the population that was negro . . . The oppression was, of course, starkly worse in the South, an area whose cherished 'way of life' was little different from South Africa's apartheid system."[46]

This same historian described the period from 1954 to 1965 as "the dawn of a new freedom." And during that period, said Mr. Evans:

> "The descendents of the slaves, who were themselves still only half free, came striding out of the shadows in the mid-1950s to claim their rightful place in the American sun."

The assault against racial discrimination was variable in form. Black veterans initiated voter registration programs. They did succeed at first in registering to vote in surprising numbers . . . an increase spread variably in Southern states was from three percent in 1940 to twelve percent by 1947. But that was of little comfort. White resistance to the black's reach for freedom was swift, visceral, and unified. The black leadership realized that appeals had to be made to all branches of government if success was to be realized. An appeal to President Truman met with modest success. Truman set up a Civil Rights Committee that came out in 1948 with a strong antidiscrimination report. The Southernbloc in Congress, in control of key committee chairmanships, made sure the rights were not secured. Truman then decreed by executive order that "equality of treatment and opportunity" in the United States Armed Forces would be a fact of life. President Eisenhower lent the moral authority of the nation to desegration by sending the troops to Arkansas to enforce the desegregation order of the Supreme Court. The intractable and visceral resistance to the freedom movement of the black Americans is graphically typified by the words of Alabama's Horace Wilkinson uttered in opposition to Trumans's 1948 campaign for the presidency: "I'd rather die fighting for state's rights than live on Truman Boulevard in nigger heaven."

The black leadership knew that to succeed, the blacks would have to unite as one in their struggle for freedom. Tiny Howard University managed to turn up an impressive legal team, including Thurgood Marshall to commence and sustain litigation in the federal courts aided by the NAACP's legal defense fund. And then there was Martin Luther King who had masterminded and spearheaded a non-violent protest against the injustices inflicted on black Americans. The non-violent movement would employ boycotts of white business merchants and massive marches on the public streets. And by this non-violent movement, King was forcing his oppressors, in his words, "to commit his brutality openly - - in the light of day - - with the rest of the world looking on." His eloquence gave character and drive to the freedom movement. What he said during the "March on Washington" stands as a monument to his goal and purpose:

> "I say to you, my friends, that in spite of the difficulties and frustrations of the moment, I still have a dream. It is a dream deeply rooted in the American dream. I have a dream that one day this nation will rise up and live out the true meaning of its creed: We hold these truths to be self-evident, that all men are created equal. I have a dream that one day on the red hills of Georgia the sons of former slaves and the sons of former slave owners will be able to sit down together at the table of brotherhood. I have a dream that one day even the state of Mississippi, a state sweltering with the heat of injustice, sweltering with the heat of oppression, will be transformed into an oasis of freedom and justice. I have a dream that my four children will one day live in a nation where they will not be judged by the color of their skin but the content of their character . . . when we allow freedom to ring, when we let it ring from every village and every hamlet, from every state and every city, we will be able to speed up that day when all of God's children, black men and white men, Jews and gentiles, Protestants and Catholics, will be able to join hands and sing in the words of the old Negro spiritual, 'Free at last!' Free at last! Thank God Almighty, we are free at last!"

The impact of the black movement on a large segment of public officials and politicians was compelling, and to some extent, extreme. It inspired in some the notion that extremism in the defense of individual rights was justified, if not by its inherent worth, then as an expiation for self-perceived failings. Such extremism spawned excesses that were never contemplated by the black movement and that would pose a threat to the nature and function of our constitutional system. This is made manifest by the subsequent notable decisions of the Supreme Court.

The 1952 case of ***Beauharnais v. Illinois,***[47] a five to four decision, raised the constitutional debate over freedom of speech to a new level of philosophic dissertation. It had all the ingredients of the power of the State versus the duty of the court, of the rights of the individual versus the interest of society and of emotional passions versus intellectual logic. It was a defining moment in the evolution of freedom of speech, as we know it today. Involved was a statute of the State of Illinois forbidding publication of,

> "Any lithograph, moving picture, play, drama or sketch, which publication or exhibition portrays depravity, criminality, unchastity, or lack of virtue of a class of citizens, of any race, color, creed or religion which said publication or exhibition exposes the citizens of any race, color, creed or religion to contempt, derision, or obloquy or which is productive of breach of the peace or riots . . ."

Beauharnais was found guilty of violating that statute and fined two hundred dollars. ***Beauharnais*** published a leaflet setting forth a petition calling on the Mayor of the City Council of Chicago,

> "to halt the further encroachment, harassment and invasion of white people, their property, neighborhoods and persons by the negro . . . if persuasion and the need to prevent the white race from becoming mongrelized by

> the negro will not unite us, then the aggressions . . . rapes, robberies, knives, guns and marijuana of the negro, surely will."

On appeal to the Supreme Court he argued that the statute deprived him of freedom of speech as guaranteed by the First Amendment. The court held that the statute did not violate his right of free speech. Supporting its decision, the court stated that the statute in question was a "form of criminal libel law," which was capable "to cause violence and disorder." Further the court noted that "No one will gainsay that it is libelous falsely to charge another with being a rapist, robber, carrier of knives and guns, and user of marijuana." In response to the argument that the statute spoke to class libel as oppose to the libel of an individual, the court said:

> "But if an utterance directed at an individual may be the object of criminal sanctions, we cannot deny to a State power to punish the same utterance directed at a define group, unless we can say that this is a wilful and purposeless restriction unrelated to the peace and well-being of the State."

The court concluded that the State of Illinois had the power to enact such legislation. In response to ***Beauharnais'*** argument that the legislation might not in practice "mitigate the evil" contemplated by the statute, the court said:

> "It is the price to be paid for the trial-and-error inherent in legislative efforts to deal with obstinate social issues. 'The science of government is the most abstruse of all

> sciences; if, indeed, that can be called a science which has but few fixed principles, and practically consists in little more than the exercise of a sound discretion, applied to the exigencies of the state as they arise. It is the science of experiment.' Anderson v. Dunn, 6 Wheat. 204, 266, 5 L.Ed. 242. Certainly the Due Process Clause does not require the legislature to be in the vanguard of science-especially sciences as young as human ecology and cultural anthropology."

The court further stated that it bears repeating,

> "that our finding that the law is not constitutionally objectionable carries no implication of approval of the wisdom of the legislation or of its efficacy. These questions may raise doubts in our minds as well as in others. It is not for us, however, to make the legislative judgment. We are not at liberty to erect those doubts into fundamental law."

Finally, the court reassured America that "while this court sits" it retains and exercises authority to nullify action which encroaches on freedom of utterance under the guise of punishing libel.

Justice Black, dissenting, registered a searing rebuke to the majority. He started his dissent by affirming that ***Beauharnais***' conviction "rest on the leaflet's <u>contents</u>, not on the time, manner and place of distribution." Justice Black then proceeded to put the issue in its factual context. He pointed out that ***Beauharnais*** was the head of an organization that opposed "amalgamation and favors segregation of white and colored people." After discussion in assembly with his group, it was decided, said Justice Black, that a petition would be submitted to the Mayor and Council of Chicago to pass laws for segregation. There was then created the pamphlet in question seeking to obtain public support for their position. Justice Black reminded that even as far back as 1689 the Bill of Rights exacted of William and Mary provided that "it is the right of the subjects to petition the King and all commitments and prosecutions for such petitioning are illegal." And 178 years ago, said Justice Black, the Declaration of Rights of the Continental Congress proclaimed to the monarch of that day that his American subjects had "a right peaceably to assemble to consider their grievances, and petition the King; and that all prosecutions, prohibitory proclamations, and commitments for the same, are illegal." After independence was won, said Justice Black, Americans adopted the First Amendment. Having said this Justice Black proclaimed:

> "Without distortion, this First Amendment could not possibly be read so as to hold that Congress has power to punish Beauharnais and others for petitioning Congress as they have here sought to petition the Chicago authorities."

The majority opinion, he complained, leaves "the rights of assembly, petition, speech, and press almost completely at the mercy of state legislative, executive and judicial agencies." But Justice Black emphasized:

> "My own belief is that no legislature is charged with the duty or vested with the power to decide what public is-

> sues Americans can discuss. In a free country that is the individual's choice, not the state's. State experimentation in curbing freedom of expression is a startling and frightening doctrine in a country dedicated to self-government by its people. I reject the holding that either state or nation can punish people for having their say in matters of public concern."

Justice Black concluded that the statute imposed state censorship over "theater, moving pictures, radio, television, leaflets, magazines, books, and newspapers." And the reach of the statute was broad enough to make criminal "many of the world's great classics, both secular and religious." He further noted that the "motives behind the state law may have been to do good."

> "But the same can be said about most laws making opinions punishable as crimes. History indicates that urges to do good have lead to the burning of books and even to the burning of 'witches.'"

In emphasizing the danger posed by the decision of the majority, Justice Black observed:

> "Today Beauharnais is punished for publicly expressing strong views in favor of segregation. Ironically enough, Beauharnais, convicted of crime in Chicago, would probably be given a hero's reception in many other localities, if not in some parts of Chicago itself. Moreover, the same kind of state law that makes Beauharnais a criminal for advocating segregation in Illinois can be utilized to send

> people to jail in other states for advocating equality and nonsegregation. What Beauharnais said in his leaflet is mild compared with usual arguments on both sides of racial controversies."

His rhetoric rising to mockery he singled out the majority's statement that freedom of petition and discussions were not in danger "while this Court sits", and said:

> "This case raises considerable doubt. Since those who peacefully petition for changes in the law are not to be protected 'while this Court sits,' who is? I do not agree that the Constitution leaves freedom of petition, assembly, speech, press or worship at the mercy of a case-by-case, day-by-day majority of this Court. I had supposed that our people could rely for their freedom on the Constitution's commands, rather than on the grace of this Court on an individual case basis."

Justice Black continued to observe that under the majority decision a valid law could be enacted to punish a candidate for President for telling the people his views. Whatever danger is perceived by the majority, Justice Black observed, "it is a danger the Founders deemed outweighed by the danger incident to the stifling of thought and speech." Sensing that the State statute in controversy was enacted as a result of pressure from the black minority, Justice Black remonstrated:

> "If there be minority groups who hail this holding as their victory, they might consider the possible relevancy of this ancient remark:

'Another such victory and I am undone.'"

Five years later, in 1957, at a time when decency and moral rectitude were still the hallmarks of society's best interest, the Supreme Court was confronted with the right of free speech versus the possession and distribution of obscene and indecent material in the case of ***Roth v. United States.***[48] One of the defendants was charged under California state statute making it a crime for keeping for sale or advertising of material that was obscene or indecent and the other was charged under a federal statute which punished the mailing of material that is obscene, lewd, lascivious and filthy or of an indecent character. The essential question presented to the court was whether or not such statute violated the right of free speech of these defendants. The Supreme Court affirmed the conviction of these defendants. But in upholding the conviction the court stated that the protection given speech and press was fashioned "to assure unfettered interchange of ideas for the bringing about of political and social changes desired by the people." Falling within the protective shelter of this aegis were "all ideas having even the slightest redeeming social importance - - unorthodox ideas, controversial ideas, even ideas hateful to the prevailing climate of opinion."

"But implicit in the history of the First Amendment is the rejection of obscenity as utterly without redeeming social importance."

In the course of the opinion, the court drew a distinction between what is obscene and what is sex. In so doing, the court stated:

> "However, sex and obscenity are not synonymous. Obscene material is material which deals with sex in a manner appealing to prurient interest. The portrayal of sex, *e. g.*, in art, literature and scientific works, is not itself suffi-

> cient reason to deny material the constitutional protection of freedom of speech and press."

The court emphasized that judging whether sex appeals to prurient interest is determined by the test:

> "Whether to the average person, applying contemporary community standards, the dominant theme of the material taken as a whole appeals to prurient interest."

This case represents a significant decision in the implementation of the political doctrine of self-government. It echoes Jefferson's philosophy of government. It recognizes the principle that the power of government originates with the people. Implicit in this decision is the recognition of the diversity of the American people. Matters of decency and morality are to be determined by the standards of the community. Under such a scheme of things moral the people of Utah are not going to be governed by the people of New York, or of Louisiana by the people of California, etc., etc. Under such a rule of law a perceived breakdown of morality in one section of America will not contaminate the morality of people in another part of America. So it was in 1957.

In 1964, in the now famous case of ***New York Times of v. Sullivan***[49], the Supreme Court worked a substantial change regarding the First Amendment free speech protection in cases of libel and commercial advertisements. It is helpful to remember that in the earlier cases already mentioned the Supreme Court had repeatedly affirmed the longstanding court decisions that libelous speech was not protected by the First Amendment. And in its earlier decision in ***Valentine v. Chrestenson*** [50], the court said that speech in commercial advertisement was not protected, even if it contained a protest against certain official action. That constitutional law was now to be changed.

In the ***New York Times*** case just mentioned, *Sullivan*, a Montgomery, Alabama Commissioner of Public Affairs, whose duties engaged him in supervising the police department, sued the New York Times newspaper, claiming he was libeled by a commercial advertisement published in the newspaper. In the advertisement, about the civil rights activities of members of the negro race including, Dr. Martin Luther King, Jr., it was stated that in their effort to uphold their constitutional guarantees, "they are being met by an unprecedented wave of terror by those who would deny and negate that document which the whole world looks upon as setting the pattern for modern freedom." It further stated that after a group of students sang "My Country Tis, of The" on the State Capitol steps, their leaders were "expelled from school, and truckloads of police armed with shot guns and tear-gas ringed the Alabama State College campus." The ad further spoke of Dr. King's peaceful protest which was met with violence, "they have bombed his home almost killing his wife and child . . ." ***Sullivan*** contended that, in his capacity as supervisor of police, he was identified as the terrorist behind such conduct and was thus grievously libeled. A jury awarded a verdict in favor of ***Sullivan*** and against the ***New York Times*** for damages. The Supreme Court reversed the decision of the state court and held that the state law authorizing such a verdict violated the First Amendment Freedom of Speech Clause and was therefore unconstitutional. In the course of its opinion the Supreme Court acknowledged that the Alabama courts had relied "on statements of this court to the effect that the Constitution does not protect libelous publications." The court, however, stated that its earlier decision did not "foreclose our inquiry here." And the reason given was that none of the cases earlier mentioned dealt with "expression critical of the official conduct of public officials." Notwithstanding earlier decisions to the contrary, the court announced that "libel can claim no talismanic immunity from constitutional limitations." Now, concluded the court, libel "must be measured by standards that satisfy the First Amendment." In support of this conclusion the court pointed out that the First Amendment's safeguard of speech was fashioned to assure "unfettered interchange of ideas for the bringing about of political and social changes desired by the people." In summarizing the court postulated:

> "Thus we consider this case against the background of a profound national commitment to the principle that debate on public issues should be uninhibited, robust, and wide-open, and that it may well include vehement, caustic, and sometimes unpleasantly sharp attacks on government and public officials."

The court further held that before a public official can recover damages for "a defamatory falsehood relating to his official conduct" he must prove that the defamatory statement was made with "actual malice– that is, with knowledge that it was false or with reckless disregard of whether it was false or not."

The court also rejected the Alabama law that made truth a defense. In rejecting it, the court concluded that compelling a critic of a public official to prove truthfulness of his critical comment would lead to a comparable "self-censorship" and this would deter criticism. Under such a rule, the court said:

> "would-be critics of official conduct may be deterred from voicing their criticism, even though it is believed to be

> true and even though it is in fact true, because of doubt whether it can be proved in court or fear of the expense of having to do so."

The court further stated that the application of the free speech provision of the First Amendment is not diminished simply because the alleged libelous statement appears in a commercial advertisement. In so doing the court stated:

> "To avoid placing such a handicap upon the freedoms of expression, we hold that if the allegedly libelous statements would otherwise be constitutionally protected from the present judgment, they do not forfeit that protection because they were published in the form of a paid advertisement."

Thus as of 1964, the First Amendment does protect libelous speech, when directed against a public official, even when contained in a commercial advertisement. And the burden is upon the public official to prove that his critic knew his statement to be false or acted in reckless disregard of its truth or falsity before damages or criminal sanctions can be imposed.

In the ***Sullivan*** case just mentioned, the Supreme Court enlarged the protection of freedom of speech of the First Amendment to include libelous speech. Five years later in ***Stanley v. Georgia*** [51] (1969), the court enlarged the freedom of speech protection of the First Amendment to include the individual's right of privacy - - "to be let alone." And under the aegis of that enlargement it proclaimed that no state law could constitutionally prohibit an individual from possessing obscene material. In other words, the court created a constitutional shelter for the individual's possession of obscene material - - material "as utterly without redeeming social importance" as declared by that same court in the 1957 ***Roth*** decision.

In the ***Stanley*** case, the defendant was charged with violating a state law of Georgia by "knowingly having possession of obscene matter" found in his house. He was convicted after jury trial of violating that state law. On appeal to the Supreme Court, ***Stanley*** argued that the Georgia statute was unconstitutional because it violated his First Amendment right of free speech. The Supreme Court agreed and reversed the conviction.

The state argued that under the Supreme Court decision in the ***Roth*** case "obscenity is not within the area of constitutionally protected speech or press." The state of Georgia, therefore, had the power to deal with such contraband material just as the state might deal with possession of other things thought to be detrimental to the welfare of its citizens. The court admitted what it had said in the ***Roth*** decision, but reasoned that the ***Stanley*** case was different. It asserted that in the ***Roth*** case, there was transmission or advertisement of the obscene material whereas in the ***Stanley*** case the material was possessed for "mere entertainment." In justifying the decision, the court further affirmed that the "right to receive information and ideas, regardless of their social worth, is fundamental to our free society." Georgia, on the contrary, asserted that exposure to obscene materials may lead to deviant sexual behavior or crimes of sexual violence. The court ultimately disposed of all of the arguments advanced by Georgia in these words:

> "Whatever may be the justifications for other statutes regulating obscenity, we do not think they reach into the pri-

> vacy of one's own home. If the First Amendment means anything, it means that a State has no business telling a man, sitting alone in his own house, what books he may read or what films he may watch. Our whole constitutional heritage rebels at the thought of giving government the power to control men's minds."

The foregoing statement exemplifies judicial high drama and soaring rhetoric. It stirs the yearning spirit of human freedom. But it can claim no talismanic immunity from scrutiny. The fact of this matter is that Georgia did not adopt its law to acquire "the power to control men's minds." It passed its law to acquire power to control men's morals. As argued to the court, Georgia adopted this law to guard against "deviant sexual behavior or crimes of sexual violence", which it thought such obscene material might excite. Georgia's perception of the detrimental effect of such obscene material was validated by subsequent history, what with the subsequent massive proliferation of the sale and distribution of pornographic pictures and films depicting children, among other things, engaged in explicit sexual activities and the concomitant sexual abuses of children by sexually perverted adults. In any event, however, in rejecting Georgia's legislative wisdom to prevent "deviant sexual behavior or crimes of sexual violence" the court said "there appears to be little empirical basis for that assertion." Disappointingly, however, the court referred to no authoritative study or source to dispute Georgia's claim. The court rejected Georgia's legislative judgment based solely on the judges' doubts about the accuracy of Georgia's legislative judgment. In so doing, however, the court turned on its head what that same court said in the 1952 ***Beauharnais*** case:

> "These questions may raise doubts in our minds as well as in others. It is not for us, however, to make the legislative judgment. We are not at liberty to erect those doubts into fundamental law."

Yet this is exactly what the ***Stanley*** court did, namely, it erected its doubts into fundamental law. Scrutiny discloses yet another concern. Accepting the court's decision that ***Stanley*** was entitled to receive obscene material it follows that the right to receive such material presupposes delivery of that material. And delivery presupposes the creation and manufacture of such obscene material. This in turn, presupposes the sale of the material by others. Thus, by approving receipt of such material the court necessarily, however unintentionally or unwittingly, encouraged the manufacture, sale and transmission of obscene material in interstate and intrastate commerce, a somewhat less than laudable notion.

Moreover, this decision told the morally loose, the sexually deviant, the sexual perverts, the worshipers of hedonism, those addicted to crass profligacy, to moral depravity, that they had the constitutional right to possess such obscene material as a means of exciting and gratifying their prurient interests. In short, they were told that moral bankruptcy is the way to go. But if the power of government originates with the people, what kind of nation can we expect to have when the power of that nation originates with such a morally depraved lot? But certainly not the type nation the founders contemplated. Our founders envisioned unalienable rights as gifts from our Creator. How could such founders create a Constitution that would enshrine degeneracy as an untouchable right? In any event, our nation was soon to learn that this judicial moral debasement would clone itself in variable ways yet to come.

Let's pause momentarily and analyze where we have been and where we appear headed under the rubric of freedom of speech. In 1942 the Supreme Court, in the ***Chaplinsky*** case, told us that allowing "the broadest scope to the language and purpose of the Fourteenth Amendment" it was well understood that "free speech is not absolute at all times and under all circumstances." There are, said the court, "certain well-defined and narrow classes of speech" that are not protected by the free speech provisions of the First Amendment. These unprotected classes of speech, "include the **lewd** and **obscene**, the **profane**, the **libelous** and the **insulting** or 'fighting words'- - those by which by their very utterance inflict injury or tend to incite an immediate breech of the peace." These classes of speech are unprotected because, declared the court, such utterances "are no essential part of any exposition of ideas, and are of such slight social value as a step to truth that any benefit that may be derived from them is clearly outweighed by the social interest in order and morality." The court quoted approvingly what was said by the Cantwell court as to such unprotected speech. The court said that "resort to epithets or personal abuse is not in any proper sense communication of information or opinion safe-guarded by the Constitution, and its punishment as a criminal act would raise no question under that instrument."

In 1952 in the ***Beauharnais*** case, the Supreme Court confirmed what it said in the ***Chaplinsky*** case, namely, that any libelous statement reflecting on the "unchastity" or on the "lack of virtues" of a class of citizens, was not protected by the freedom of speech provisions of the First Amendment and was subject to criminal prosecution.

In 1957 in the ***Roth*** case the Supreme Court declared that anyone mailing or possessing for sale any obscene material could be criminally prosecuted, because the freedom of speech provision of the First Amendment did not protect such conduct or speech. The court even defined obscenity it said "obscene material is material which deals with sex in a manner appealing to prurient interest." And person charged with such conduct would be judged by what the "average person" applying "contemporary community standards, as to whether or not the material taken as a whole "appeals to prurient interest."

In the 1964 ***Sullivan*** decision we witness the Supreme Court engaging in the act of disinterring the cadaver of the constitutional principle of libelous speech and breathing into its nostril a new life all its own. As a result, libel, theretofore thought to be of "such slight social value as a step to truth" as to be unprotected by the right to free speech, now was raised to new constitutional high ground. Now, said the court, libel "must be measured by standards that satisfy the First Amendment."

And now in 1969, the ***Stanley*** court tells America that one has the constitutional right to receive obscene material, reversing its earlier decision to the effect that "obscenity is not within the area of constitutionally protected speech or press." We witness the court enshrining degeneracy as an untouchable constitutional right of the individual.

The ***Stanley*** decision was followed by the 1971 decision in ***Cohen v. California.*** [52] ***Cohen*** was convicted of violating the California Penal Code which prohibits "maliciously and willfully disturbing the peace or quiet of any neighborhood or person - - by - - offensive conduct" and was sentenced to thirty days in prison. The essential facts of the case are to the effect that defendant was observed in the Los Angeles County Courthouse in the corridor outside of Division 20 of the municipal court, wearing a jacket bearing the words "Fuck the Draft", which were plainly visible. There were women and children present in the corridor. ***Cohen*** defended the accusation by asserting that he wore the jacket knowing that the words were on the jacket as a means of informing the public of the depth of his feelings against the Vietnam war and the draft. In affirming ***Cohen's*** conviction, the California Court of Appeal held that the "offensive conduct" of the Penal Code means "behavior which has a tendency to provoke others to acts of violence or to in turn disturb the peace." That state court concluded that it was "certainly reasonably foreseeable that such conduct might cause others to rise up to commit a violent act against the person of the defendant or attempt to forcibly remove his jacket."

The Supreme Court stated that the issue before it was whether California could excise "one particular scurrilous epithet from the public discourse, either upon the theory of the court below that its use is inherently likely to cause violent reaction" or on the more general assertion that California could "properly remove this offensive word from the public vocabulary." This, the court said California could not do because of the freedom of speech guaranteed by the First Amendment. In rationalizing its decision, the majority opinion concluded, "this is not, for example, an obscenity case,"

> "Whatever else may be necessary to give rise to the States' broader power to prohibit obscene expression, such expression must be, in some significant way, errotic."

While conceding that the First Amendment does not protect so called "fighting words" the court concluded that no individual could "reasonably have regarded the words on appellant's jacket as a direct personal insult." Further, the court reasoned that the constitutional right of free expression "is powerful medicine in a society as diverse and populous as ours." That freedom is intended, continued the court, "to remove governmental restraints from the arena of public discussion" and not allowing government to decide what views shall be voiced. Further reasoned the court "so long as the means are peaceful, the communication need not meet standards of acceptability." Finally the court concluded:

> "For, while the particular four-letter word being litigated here is perhaps more distasteful than most others of its genre, it is nevertheless often true that one man's vulgarity is another's lyric."

Linguistic expression, however vulgar, the court concluded, "serves a dual communicative function" in addition to conveying ideas, it also conveys "inexpressible emotions" as well.

Thus by 1971 we witness the court discovering yet another species of speech, protected by the First Amendment: rebaldry and vulgarity. As it rationalized its conclusion, the court discovered a speech dichotomy. It asserted that "linguistic expression" (speech) serves a "dual communicative function." It conveys, said the court, "relatively precise, detached explications" and also "inexpressible emotions." In fact, the court postulated, "words are often chosen as much for their emotive as their cognitive force." Moreover, intoned the court, emotive speech "may often be the more important element of the overall message sought to be communicated." In other words, vulgar and ribald speech "may often be" the more important method of effective speech. If so, however, such a view means that self-restraint in speech induced by self-respect and personal dignity falls short of the speech contemplated by the First Amendment. This in turn means that the court now is telling us that in order for everybody to enjoy freedom of public speech contemplated by the First Amendment, the standard of such public speech must be lowered so as to include vulgar speech. This is so because we must make allowance for "inexpressible emotions." Inexpressible emotions mean that man has emotions which meaningful words cannot express; therefore, man must be allowed to use words to express his "inexpressible emotion." Inexpressible words are the stuff that babble is made of. Webster's Dictionary describes babble: "to say indistinctively or incoherently; to say foolishly or inadvisedly; confused, incoherent talk or vocal sounds; foolish or meaningless talk." Thus the decision of the court tells us that the First Amendment contemplates the establishment of a tower of babble. Included among the genre of "Fuck the Draft" are such emotive words as "fuck you", "mother fucker", etc, etc. Who, in his wildest imagination, could believe that the founders of our nation, who believed in the existence of a supreme being, ever contemplated that the First Amendment would protect such vulgarity and ribaldry as a concomitant of public speech?

This decision is a classic example of the court tolerating public speech more by respecting it less. That is the culture and philosophy of secular humanism, a humanism defined by Webster's Dictionary as a "modern, nontheistic, rationalist movement that holds that man is capable of self-fulfillment, ethical conduct, etc., without recourse to supernaturalism." This depicts the self as unencumbered by any traditional or cultural values, and represents a radical departure from the free speech formula solemenly articulated by the court in its 1942 decision in the ***Chaplinsky*** case. It will be recalled that ***Chaplinsky's*** conviction was approved by the Supreme Court for publically telling another citizen that "you are a God damned racketeer and a damned fascist and the whole government of Rochester are fascists." In that case the court concluded that such speech was not protected by the First Amendment, because it fell within the "narrowly limited classes of speech the punishment of which has never been thought to raise constitutional problem." Such prohibited speech, the court stated, "include the **lewd** and **obscene**, the **profane**, **libelous**, and **insulting** or **fighting words** -those which by there very utternace inflict injury or tend to incite an immediate breech of the peace." Thus what was vulgar and lewd in 1942 was in 1971 "another's lyric."

And oh what lyrics we have reaped! The lyrics of rock and roll music, targeting preteenage and teenage children, are so violent in nature, so sexually perverted and so morally depraved as to have created national alarm for the safety and welfare of today's (1998) children. Without available legal recourse, because the Supreme Court has decided that vulgarity (lyrics) is speech protected by the Constitution, parents can but abjectly implore the music industry and the so-called artists to exercise self-restraint and to agree to put warning labels on their music to give parents the remote opportunity to guide their children away from such vile lyrics, and protect them against the slim of such degeneracy. The parents'effete effort to protect their children has engaged them in organizing what is called Parents Music Resource Center. It was organized in May of 1998. At a meeting of this organization in 1998, Mrs. Tipper Gore, wife of Vice-President Gore, was one of the speakers. The purpose of the meeting was stated by Mrs. Gore: "We are asking the recording industry to voluntarily assist parents who are concerned by placing a warning label on music products inappropriate for younger children due to explicit sexual or violent lyrics." She also said that they were asking that "lyrics for labeled music products be available to the consumer before purchased in the marketplace." Mrs. Gore futher stated:

> "We are simply asking that these corporate and artistic rights be exercised with responsibility, with sensitivity, and some measure of self-restraint, especially since young minds are at stake. We are talking about preteenagers and young teenagers having access to this material."

After Mrs. Gore's short remarks she turned the program over to a Mr. Ling, who was nominated to present a "presentation to acquaint you with the type of material that is in question." In characterizing the material in question, Mr. Ling said:

> "Today the element of violent, brutal erotica, has exploded in rock music in an unprecedented way. Many albums today include songs that encourage suicide, violent revenge, sexual violence, and violence just for violence's sake."

In the course of his remarks, and in showing samples of the lyrics, he pointed out that just a few days before his appearance two young teenagers committed suicide while listening to the lyrics of the song "Shoot to Thrill." He predicted that some "6,000 will take their lives this year." And he said many of these people find encouragement from some rock stars who "present death as a positive, almost attractive alternative." Then he gave examples. In the album called "Fade to Black" there exists the following lyric "I have lost the will to live, Simply nothing more to give. There is nothing more for me. I need the end to set me free." He then referred to the song "Whiplash":

> "Bang your head against the stage like you never have before. Make it rain, make it bleed, make it really sore.

> In a frenzied madness, now is the time to let it rip, to let it fucking loose. We are gathered here to maim and kill, for this is what we choose."

Then he quoted the lyrics from the song "Shoot them Down":

> "They think we are fools who want to make their own rules. It only gets us madder. They think they are hot. Well, I say they're not. They shoot us down for fun. If they don't want to play, then let's make them pay. Shoot them down with a fucking gun."

Witness the following lyric from the album "Back in Business":

> "Don't you struggle or try to bite. You want some trouble, I am the king of vice. I am a wrecking ball. I am a stinging knife. Steal your money. Going to take your life."

And from the song "Eat Me Alive" Judas Priest sings:

> "Squealing in passion as the rod of steel injects. Gut wrenching frenzy that deranges every joint. I am going to force you at gunpoint to eat me alive."

And from the album "On Their Knees," the band Great White sings these words:

> "Knocking down your door, going to pull you to the floor, taking what I choose, never going to lose, going to drive my love inside you, going to nail your ass to the floor."

From their song "Bastard" the Motley Crue sing out:

"Out goes the light. In goes my knife. Pull out his life. Consider the bastard dead."

The Piledriver band sings this lyric in the song "Lust":

"Hell on fire. Lust, desire. The devil wants to stick you. The devil wants to you. He wants your body. He wants your spirit. Naked twisting bodies, sweating. Prince of darkness. Prince of evil. Spread your legs and scream. This is no dream. Degradation. Humiliation. Thrusting, shoving. Animal humping. He is like a dog in heat. You are just another piece of meat. Craving demons fill you with pain. Now you are bloodied and stained, hurt and beaten. He will possess you. He will molest you. Sex with Satan. Sex with Satan."

Then there is this song from Purple Rain, the multimillion seller by Prince, which presents this lyric from the song "Darling Nikki":

"I met a girl named Nikki. I guess you could say she was a sex fiend. I met her in a hotel lobby masturbating with magazines."

Here is a lyric of the song "Sister":

"I was only 16, but I guess that is no excuse. My sister was 32, and kind of alone. My sister never made love to anyone but me. Incest is everything it's said to be."

And from the album "Cock Rock Shock" the words are:

"We are going to fuck you" and "Oh, you fucking little

bitch."

And from the album of the band KISS there is included songs such as "Fits Like a Glove," whose lyrics are:

> "Ain't a cardinal sin, baby. Let me in. Girl I am going to treat you right. Well, goodness sakes, my snake's alive, and it is ready to bite. Baby, let me in. It fits like a glove. I think I am going to burst. When I go through her it is like a hot knife through butter."

And from the song "Give Me More":

> "Hot blood, need your love. Hard as rock, can't get enough. Want to feel you deep inside, pumping through my veins. Fill you to the cord, like a dog to the bone. Make you sweat, make you moan. Come on, lick my candy cane."

Mr. Ling emphasizes that the "list is endless." He is quoted as saying that the album released by the band Mentors, included songs like "Four-F Club," "Find Her, Feel Her, Fuck Her, and Forget Her," "Free Fix for a Fuck," "Clap Queen," "My Erection is Over," and the song "Golden Showers," which says these words, "Listen you little slut, do as you are told, come with daddy for me to pour the gold. Golden showers. All through my excrement you shall roam. Bend up and smell my anal vapor. Your face is my toilet paper. On your face I leave a shit tower. Golden showers."

PMRC reports that since the sale of such songs "teenage pregnancy and teenage suicide rates are at epidemic proportions today (1998)."

Further rape is up 7% "in the latest statistics." And the "suicide rates of youth between 16 and 24 has gone up 300% in the last three decades (since the Supreme Court decision in the ***Cohen's*** case), while the adult level has remained the same." Thus, this is the type of speech unleashed upon our society as a result of being made legitimate by the Sureme Court decision in the ***Cohen*** case.

Tagging along with the development of emotive speech is the concept of symbolic speech, that is, conduct which implies a message, as a species of speech protected by the First Amendment. The concept of symbolic speech found roots in the early 1960s. Examples of the symbolic speech declared by the court as protected by the First Amendment include the wearing of black armbands worn by students in public school as a protest against United States policy in Vietnam war; sit-in by Negro students in "whites only" libraries to protest segregation; flying a red flag as a gesture of support for communism; displaying a United States flag with a peace symbol attached to it and burning the American flag. Distinguishing conduct from speech and disagreement over the question of whether or not the conduct implies speech readily understood by the average citizens were sources of judicial controversies. The only constant aspect of such controversies in the legal conclusion that some conduct implies some message rising to the level of protected speech. The 1984 case of ***Clark v. Community for Creative Non-Violence*** [53] exemplifies both the controversy regarding what is or not protected conduct and the inherent controversy which such conduct excites.

The issue involved in that case was whether the National Park Service regulation prohibiting camping in certain parts of the national capital violated the First Amendment right of demonstrators. The regulation in question prohibited demonstrators from sleeping in Lafayette Park and the Mall, in connection with a demonstration intended to call attention to the plight of the homeless. The park service however authorized the erection of two symbolic ten cities: twenty tents in Lafayette Park that would accommodate fifty people and forty tents in the Mall with a capacity of up to one hundred. But the Park Service specifically denied the demonstrators' request that they be permitted to sleep in the symbolic tents. These demonstrators contended that this regulation, preventing sleeping in the tents, violated their First Amendment right of free speech. The federal district court ruled in favor of the Park Service. The Court of Appeal, sitting en banc, reversed the district court. The eleven judges of the appellate court produced six opinions. Six of the eleven judges concluded that the regulation infringed the demonstrators' First Amendment right by denying them of the right sleep in the tents. But the other five judges agreed with the opinion of the District Court. The Supreme Court reversed the decision of the Court of Appeal and held that the regulation was constitutionally permitted. In the course of the opinion the court reminded that free speech "whether oral or written or symbolized by conduct" is always subject to "reasonable time, place, or manner restrictions." Such restrictions, the court postulated, are valid provided that:

> "They are justified without reference to the content of the regulated speech, that they are narrowly tailored to serve a significant governmental interest, and that they leave open ample alternative channels for communication of the information."

While sleeping in the tents may be expressive and part of the message of the demonstration, the act of sleeping in the tents, said the court, reflected the element of the "manner" of the expression and therefore subject to the regulation in controversy. The court concluded also that the regulation was "content-neutral" because it was not being applied as a "disagreement with the message presented." The court also held that the government had a substantial interest "in maintaining the parks in the heart of our Capital in an attractive and intact condition, readily available to the millions of people who wish to see and enjoy them by their presence."

Chief Justice Burger concurred with the majority opinion. He agreed with the opinion but for different reasons. His position was that the demonstrators' attempt "at camping in the park" was essentially "conduct, not speech." It was his view that the demonstrators' insistence that camping was protected speech only "trivializes" the First Amendment of free speech. Exhibiting judicial impatience the Chief Justice further remonstrated:

> "And it tells us something about why many people must wait for their 'day in court' when the time of the courts is pre-empted by frivolous proceedings that delay the causes of litigants who have legitimate, nonfrivolous claims. This case alone has engaged the time of 1 District Judge, an en banc court of 11 Court of Appeals judges, and 9 Justices of this Court."

Justice Marshall, the NAACP's civil rights ex-warrior, joined by Justice Brennan, vigorously dissented. The essence of the dissent verbalized by Justice Marshall is as follows:

> "The primary purpose for making *sleep* and integral part of the demonstration was 'to re-enact the central reality

> of homelessness,' and to impress upon public consciousness, in as dramatic way as possible, that homelessness is a widespread problem, often ignored, that confronts its victims with life-threatening deprivations."

Thus it is evident that symbolic speech, as with emotive speech, is flawed with such inherent imprecision as to make men of common intelligence guess as to what is protected and what is not, and as to make the common claims of free speech but a trivialization of the First Amendment to some judges and a fundamental constitutional breech to others. In that context "content-neutrality" is but a fiction to make plausible to some that which is but fallacious to others. And such an inherent difference is insoluble. It is insoluble because symbols are but implications of conduct. And by definition implication is the antithesis of precision of meaning. The process of searching for its meaning engages the inquirer in roaming about in the domain of his knowledge, his experiences, his sensitivities, his preferences, and his predilections. Such symbols are, therefore, incapable of standardization, except those by common consent that are deeply rooted in the traditions of a people. Common sense informs us that verbal speech is sufficiently precise in meaning and elastic in application to provide adequate protection to the First Amendment right of free speech of our citizens. It is inviting moral and civic anemia to rely upon the moral degeneracy of emotive speech and the chaotic vagaries of symbolic speech as agencies to vindicate the First Amendment right of free speech.

By 1991 the 1957 decision of the Supreme Court in the ***Roth*** case appeared to be but an archeological decaying fossil. Even its carbon emission now was morally vapid. It is well to recall that the ***Roth*** case involved the criminal conviction of the defendant for possessing "obscene" material. ***Roth*** argued that the First Amendment entitled him to possess such obscene material. The Supreme Court disagreed. In so doing it said:

> "Implicit in the history of the First Amendment is the rejection of obscenity as utterly without redeeming social importance."

Moreover, the court defined obscene material as:

> "material which deals with sex in a manner appealing to prurient interest."

And of equal significance the court declared that whether or not the material appealed to prurient interest was to be determined by "community standards," saying:

> "Whether to the average person, applying contemporary community stands, the dominant theme of the material taken as a whole appeals to prurient interest."

But since the ***Roth*** decision, the Supreme Court has recognized for example, nude dancing as an expressive activity protected by the free speech clause of the First Amendment, even though such activity presented a message of eroticism, that eroticism identified by the court in the ***Roth*** decision as "obscene." In fact the Supreme Court has stamped the free speech imprimatur of the First Amendment on commercial enterprises who deal in nothing but pornographic material, including movie films, whose sole purpose is to excite the prurient interest of the viewer, notwithstanding the vigorous and repetitive protest of citizens speaking thrugh their state government. One of the latest protests against nudity was made by the State of Indiana and considered by the Supreme Court in the 1991 case of ***Barnes v. Glen Theatre, Inc.,*** [54]

Indiana state law prohibited nude dancing and required that dancers had to wear "pasties" and "G-strings" when dancing. Nude entertinment establishments in South Bend, Indiana wanted to present "totally nude dancing" by their females engaged in "go-go dancing." They argued that nude dancing was a "symbolic speech" and therefore protected by the First Amendment and the Indiana law, to the extent that it prohibited such nude dancing, was unconstitutional. The court rejected such a claim and held that the Indiana statute was constitutionally permissible. The court's effort to rationalize its decision in the context of its earlier decisions engaged it in a venture of intellectual agony. Its rationale is a lesson in semanticism and sophistry of the highest order. For example, the parties attacking the validity of the Indiana law argued that by prohibiting the performance of nude dancing, Indiana sought to "prevent its erotic message," that is, the speech element of the dancing activity. This, they argued, could not be done because the Supreme Court had earlier ruled in many cases that governmental interest in suppressing speech "must be unrelated to the suppression of free expression." In other words, these parties were saying that the sole purpose of the Indiana law requiring dancers to wear "pasties" and "G-strings" was to reduce the impact of the erotic message of nude dancing. And in turn, since the sole purpose of nude dancing is to express an "erotic message" the state law denied the dancers of their First Amendment right of free speech. That was seemingly an impregnable argument. For starters, how was one to extirpate the genital organs of the dancers from their nude bodies by covering them, while simultaneously arguing that such an act was not designed to impair the excitement of the prurient interest of the viewers? Without even the slightest indication of blushing, the court maintained the constitutionality of the Indiana statute in these words:

> "the requirement that the dancers don pasties and G-strings does not deprive the dance of whatever erotic message it conveys; it simply makes the message slightly less graphic. The perceived evil that Indiana seeks to address is not erotic dancing, but public nudity. The appearance of people of all shapes, sizes and ages in the nude at a beach, for example, would convey little if any erotic message, yet the State still seeks to prevent it. Public nudity is the evil the State seeks to prevent, whether or not it is combined with expressive activity."

Justice Scalia agreed with the decision but for different reason. He summarized his position in these words:

> "In my view, however, the challenged regulation must be upheld, not because it survives some lower level of First Amendment scrutiny, but because, as a general law regulating conduct and not specifically directed at expression, it is not subject to First Amendment scrutiny at all."

Justices White, Marshall, Blackmun and Stevens dissented. In the course of this dissent, Justice White said:

> "That the performances in the Kitty Kat Lounge may not be high art, to say the least, and may not appeal to the Court, it is hardly an excuse for distorting and ignoring

> settled doctrine. The court's assessment of the artistic merits of nude dancing performances should not be the determining factor in deciding this case."

In the course of that dissent, the language of the court in ***Cohen*** decision was approvingly invoked:

> "[W]hile the entertainment afforded by a nude ballet at Lincoln Center to those who can pay the price may differ vastly in content (as viewed by judges) or in quality (as viewed by critics), it may not differ in substance from the dance viewed by the person who...wants some 'entertainment' with his beer or shot of rye."

This case finds the court drowning in its own decisions. Such judicial chaos exists because, in giving vent to their political agendas in the past, our Supreme Court judges have blurred the marked distinction between art and obscenity, between humanism and supernaturalism, and have been disloyal to the founding notion that we are a nation "under God" where the unalienable rights of our citizens are gifts form God and not from man.

By 1998 judicial neutralism by use of its nihilistic sword had so neutralized all forms of speech of its moral content that the concept of "decency and respect" no longer retained any indigenous cognitive relevance. The liberal moralists looked upon such concept as but a naive notion used to beguile the ignorant and as a device used by the moral majority to manipulate their followers. It was, these liberal moralists said, an ancient relic alien to the enlightened notion of humanism.

The National Endowment for the Arts (NEA), a federal agency created by Congress in 1965, is an example of how neutralism works. The NEA was created by Congress as a "broadly conceived national policy for the arts in the Unites States," pledging federal funds to "help create and sustain not only a climate encouraging freedom of thought, imagination, and inquiry but also the material conditions facilitating the release of . . .creative talent." The enabling statute invested the NEA with substantial discretion to "award grants" to support persons involved in activities of "artistic and cultural significance, giving emphasis to American creativity and cultural diversity, professional excellence" and for the encouragement of "public knowledge, education, understanding, and appreciation of the arts." Applications for NEA funding are initially reviewed by advisory panels composed of supposed experts in the relevant field of the arts. In 1989 the NEA funded Robert Mapplethorpe's work. To support his work he was granted $30,000.00. His work was entitled "The Perfect Moment" and it included "homoerotic photographs that several members of Congress condemned as pornographic." The NEA also granted $15,000.00 to Andres Serrano. With this money Serrano produced a work which he entitled "Piss Christ." It was a photograph of a crucifix immersed in urine. Thus taxpayer's funds were used by the NEA to support these two projects, which were considered by the NEA as words of "artistic and cultural significance" and ranked as "professional excellence," in order to encourage "public knowledge, education, understanding and appreciation of the arts." As the Supreme Court later pointed out "when considering the NEA's appropriations for fiscal year 1990, Congress reacted to the controversy surrounding the Mapplethorpe and Serrano photographs by eliminating $45,000.00 from the agency's budget, the precise amount contributed to the two exhibits by NEA grant recipients." In the final draft of the 1990 amendment, Congress created a provision that directed the NEA, when establishing procedures to judge the artistic merit of grant application, to:

> "Take into consideration general standards of decency and respect for the diverse beliefs and values of the American public."

After this amendment came into effect, four individuals considered to be "performance artists" applied for NEA grants. A majority of the NEA council recommended disapproval and the NEA subsequently informed these individuals that they had been denied funding. These individuals filed a lawsuit claiming that applying the "standards of decency and respect" infringed upon their right of free speech and that therefore this amendment was unconstitutional. ***National Endowment For the Arts v. Finley.*** [55] The federal district court agreed with this argument, and so did the Court of Appeal. In declaring the amendment unconstitutional the district court asserted that,

> "the very nature of our pluralistic society is that there are an infinite number of values and beliefs, and correlatively, there may be no national 'general standard of decency.'"

In agreeing the Court of Appeal concluded that,

> "decency and respect criteria are not susceptible to objective definition."

One of the judges of the appellate court dissented and asserted that the First Amendment "protects artists' rights to express themselves as indecently and disrespectfully as they like, but does not compel the Government to fund that speech."

The Supreme Court reversed the decision of the lower courts and held that the requirement of "decency and respect" was constitutionally enforceable. Justice O'Connor delivered the opinion of the court. Justice Ginsberg joined the majority opinion in part. Justice Scalia filed an opinion concurring with the majority opinion in which Justice Thomas joined. Justice Souter filed a dissenting opinion. In substance the majority opinion held that "decency" is a "permissible factor where educational suitability motivates its consideration." While the majority opinion reversed the lower courts, the opinion suffers from excessive judicial timidity. This view is captured by Justice Scalia's opening statement:

> "'The operation was a success, but the patient died.' What such a procedure is to medicine, the Court's opinion in this case is to law. It sustains the constitutionality of 20 U.SC. § 954 (d)(1) by gutting it. The most avid congressional opponents of the provision could not have asked for more. I write separately because, unlike the Court, I think that § 954 (d)(1) must be evaluated as written, rather than as distorted by the agency it was meant to control. By its terms, it establishes content-and viewpoint-based criteria upon which grant application are to be evaluated. <u>And that is perfectly constitutional.</u>"

Justice Scalia pointedly declared that the amendment regarding "decency and respect" reflected a congressional rebellion against the offensive productions of the two "performance artists." Said Justice Scalia:

> "It is evident in the legislative history that § 954 (d)(1) was prompted by, and directed at, the public funding of

> such offensive productions as Serrano's 'Piss Christ,' the portrayal of a crucifix immersed in urine, and Mapplethorpe's show of lurid homoerotic photographs."

Lamenting the circumlocution of the majority opinion Justice Scalia observed:

> "Thus, even if one strays beyond the plain text it is perfectly clear that the statute was meant to disfavor — that is, to discriminate against — such productions."

In rationalizing the constitutional validity of this amendment Justice Scalia postulated:

> "Congress did not abridge the speech of those who disdain the beliefs and values of the American public, nor did it abridge indecent speech. Those who wish to create indecent and disrespectful art are as unconstrained now as they were before the enactment of this statute. *Avant-garde artistes* such as respondents remain entirely free to *epater les bourgeois*; they are merely deprived of the additional satisfaction of having the bourgeoisie taxed to pay for it."

To realize that a law which seeks to create space in the artistic world by requiring compliance with the concept of "decency and respect" should excite such a monumental controversy speaks convincingly of the degree to which America has undergone moral decline. At the same time this decision shows that there is light at the end of this tunnel of moral indifference. It shows that, given congressional courage and principled judges, the return to the founding values of our nation is reachable; that America may once again belong to we the people where the power of government originates.

CHAPTER TEN

THE RIGHT OF PRIVACY
THE GENESIS OF ABORTION

Evolution and Nature of the Right of Privacy

The first notable stirring in legal circles of the right of privacy, as we now know it, occurred in 1890, in an article entitled "The Right of Privacy," published in the Harvard Law Review by Samuel Warren and Louis Brandeis, then a Boston lawyer. (Mr. Brandeis, a republican, later in 1916 at age 59 was appointed to the Supreme Court by President Wilson and served until 1939.) The article was inspired by Warren's annoyance at press coverage of the lavish entertainment he conducted in his home in Boston's elite Black Bay. In part pertinent, the article said:

> "The press is overstepping in every direction the obvious bound of propriety and decency. Gossip is no longer the resource of the idle and of the various, but has become a

> trade, which is pursued with industry as well as effrontery. To satisfy a prurient taste the details of sexual relations are spread broadcast in the columns of the daily papers. To occupy the indolent column upon which is filled with idle gossip, which can only be procured by intrusion upon the domestic circle."

The authors further complained that such indiscretion brought "a lowering of social standards and of morality" and infringed the "right of the individual to be let alone." This article was adumbrative of an unprecedented expansion of the concept of the privacy rights of citizens.

It is apparent that Messers, Warren and Brandeis were inspired by the earlier 1886 decision of the Supreme Court in ***Boyd v. United States*** [56], to make their statement extending the extant reach of personal liberty. They obviously took serious note of Lord Camden's opinion (referred to in the ***Boyd*** opinion) in the 1765 case of ***Entick v. Carrington***, 19 How.St.Tr. 1029:

> "The principles laid down in this opinion affect the very essence of constitutional liberty and security. They reach further than the concrete form of the case then before the court, with its adventitious circumstances; they apply to all invasions on the part of the government and its employees of the sanctity of a man's home and the privacies of life. It is not the breaking of his doors, and the rummaging of his drawers, that constitutes the essence of the offense; but it is the invasion of his indefeasible right of personal security, personal liberty, and private property, where that right has never been forfeited by his convic-

> tion of some public offense, -it is the invasion of his sacred right which underlies and constitutes the essence of Lord Camden's judgment."

Thus, as far back as 1886, the Supreme Court held that the liberty guaranteed by the Constitution guarded more that a man's home from government intrusion, it guarded "the privacies of life." While ***Boyd*** was decided within the factual context of an illegal government seizure, the Court based its opinion not merely on the narrow right to be free from unlawful seizure, but upon the right of all citizens to be free and secure in the "privacies" of their lives. It was the government's "invasion of [the] indefeasible right of personal security" which led the Court to invalidate the seizure. This seminal concept of privacy, though not necessary to support the ***Boyd*** decision, was to work its way through a labyrinth of truculent social, moral and political issues to finally produce the controversial constitutional right of a female to kill a developing human being in her womb, which has spawned bitter division and violence not witnessed in this country since the debate on slavery.

Before taking off from the launch pad regarding the right of privacy, a notable historic note must be recalled. While the ***Boyd*** decision was rendered in 1886, and the Fourteenth Amendment was ratified in July of 1868, some eighteen (18) years before the ***Boyd*** decision, the Fourteenth Amendment was not made applicable against the states until 1897, some eleven (11) years after ***Boyd.*** It is pertinent to recall that the first time the Supreme Court considered the legal effect of the Fourteenth Amendment was in the Louisiana ***Slaughterhouse*** case decided by the Supreme Court in 1873. In that case the more the majority scrutinized the numerosity of rights included within the generic term "privileges and immunities" of the Fourteenth Amendment, the more incredible it appeared to their minds that the Fourteenth Amendment was ever intended to confer upon the Supreme Court such awesome power over the states. The majority underscored their judicial doubt stating that, if true, the Supreme Court would be established as:

> " . . .a perpetual censor upon all legislations of the states, on the civil rights of their own citizens, with authority to nullify such as it did not approve as consistent with those rights, as they existed at the time of the adoption of this amendment . . ."

The Supreme Court concluded that such a broad sweep so overwhelmingly subjected the states to the control of the federal government as to make its application to the states inconsistent with the fundamental spirit and structure of the relationship between the federal government and state governments. In effect the court acknowledged that the national government existed only as a sovereign of power delegated to it by the states. In short, the tail was never intended to wag the dog. Said the court:

> "But when, as in the case before us, these consequences are so serious, so far-reaching and pervading, so great a departure from the structure and spirit of our institutions; when the effect is to fetter and degrade the state governments by subjecting them to the control of Congress, in the exercise of powers heretofore universally conceded to them of the most ordinary and fundamental character; when in fact it radically changes the whole theory relations of the state and federal government to each other

> and of both these governments to the people; the argument has a force that is irresistible, in the absence of language which expresses such a purpose too clearly to admit of doubt.
>
> We are convinced that no such results were intended by the Congress which proposed these amendments, nor by the Legislatures of the state which ratified them."

But there was dissent among the justices. Justice Field characterized the dissent in these words:

> "The question presented is therefore, one of the gravest importance not merely to the parties here, but to the whole country. It is nothing less than the question whether the recent amendments to the federal constitution protect the citizens of the United States against the deprivation of their common rights by state legislation. In my judgment, the Fourteenth Amendment does afford such protection and was so intended by the Congress which framed and the states which adopted it."

The purpose of the adoption of the Fourteenth Amendment, said Justice Field was to:

> "place the common rights of American citizens under the protection of the national government."

The rights contemplated by the Fourteenth Amendment were identified by Justice Field in these words:

> "That amendment was intended to give practical effect to the declaration of 1776 of unalienable rights, **rights which are the gift of the Creator; which the law does not confer but only recognizes**."

But in 1897 the Supreme Court reversed itself in the case of ***Allgeyer v. State of Louisiana***. [57] And in reversing itself the minority opinion of the ***Slaughterhouse Case*** became the majority opinion in the ***Allgeyer*** case. The Supreme Court stated emphatically that indeed that which was considered unintended by the ***Slaughterhouse*** court was in fact the intention of the Fourteenth Amendment; that the Supreme Court was conferred the power to be a "perpetual censor upon all legislations of the state, on the civil rights of their own citizens" with authority to nullify any state law that deprives state citizens of their "unalienable" rights. In assessing the reach of the "unalienable" rights of the declaration of independence, and contemplated by the Fourteenth Amendment, the court enumerated these rights as follows:

> "The 'liberty' mentioned in that amendment means, not only the right of the citizen to be free from the mere physical restraint of his person, as by incarceration, but the term is deemed to embrace the right of the citizen to be free in the enjoyment of all his faculties; to be free to use them in all lawful ways; to live and work where he wills; to earn his livelihood by any lawful calling; to pursue any livelihood or avocation; and for that purpose to enter into all contracts which may be proper, necessary, and essential to his carrying out to a successful conclusion the purposes above mentioned."

The Fourteenth Amendment, fueled by such a concept of liberty, was destined to become the legal juggernaut that would be used to define a tortured implementation of the "unalienable" rights of our citizens to include secular and materialistic notions at war with the religious nature of our charter of freedom. But back to the evolution.

In April, 1919, Nebraska passed a law prohibiting any person from teaching any subject to any person in any language other than the English language where the pupil shall not have attained and successfully passed the "Eighth Grade." One Robert Meyer was tried and convicted of violating this state law by teaching the German language to a pupil who had not passed the eighth grade. The state court held that the purpose of the law was to prevent children of foreigners who emigrated to the country from being taught from early childhood the language of their country "so that they must always think in that language, and, as a consequence, naturally inculcate in them the ideas and sentiments foreign to the best interest of this country." Nebraska wanted the English language to "become the mother tongue of all children reared in this state." The Supreme Court disagreed and held such a state law violated the Fourteenth Amendment to the Constitution. ***Meyer v. State of Nebraska***, (1923).[58] In that case, the court pointed out that the Fourteenth Amendment expressly provided that no state "shall deprive any person of life, liberty or property without due process of law." The court concluded that while the court had not attempted to define "with exactness" the liberty guaranteed, the court concluded:

> "Without doubt, it denotes not merely freedom from bodily restraint but also the right of the individual to contact, to engage in any of the common occupations of life, to ac-

> quire useful knowledge, to marry, establish a home and bring up children, to worship God according to the dictates of his own conscience, and generally to enjoy those privileges long recognized at common law as essential to the orderly pursuit of happiness by free men."

The court emphasized that the American people have "always regarded education and acquisition of knowledge as matter of supreme importance which should be diligently promoted. Defendant ***Meyer's*** right to "teach and the right of parents to engage him so to instruct their children" fall within the liberty concept of the Fourteenth Amendment. The court observed that the unfortunate experiences "during the late war" (World War I) apparently motivated this state law. But the court said the adoption of that law exceeded the limitations upon the "power of the state" to adopt the law because it conflicted with "rights assured" to the defendant and parents of the children involved and thus existed in violation of the Fourteenth Amendment.

The ***Meyer*** decision was followed by the 1925 decision in the case of ***Pierce v. Society of the Sisters of the Holy Names, et al.*** [59] The state of Oregon adopted a law which required compulsory education of children between the ages of 8 and 16 years in a "public school," and failure to do so resulted in the imposition of criminal sanctions. The Society of Sisters, a private corporation, engaged in educating children in both temporal and religious courses, attacked the state law as existing in violation of the Fourteenth Amendment in that it took from this private corporation the right to engage in the lawful business of conducting educational schools. The court agreed with this argument and held that the state law was unreasonable and constituted an unlawful interference with and the destruction of the property interest of this school corporation without due process and in violation of the Fourteenth Amendment. The Supreme Court thus held that a state could not deprive this corporation of the right to engage in its business enterprise because of its right of privacy to engage in lawful business.

It is 1928, 38 years after ***Brandeis***, the Boston lawyer, joined his law partner, Samuel Warren, in writing their article in the Harvard Law Review regarding "The Right of Privacy" complaining about the newspaper publication of the lavish entertainment conducted in Warren's home in Boston's elite Black Bay. In that article, it will be recalled, they complained that such publication infringed the "right of the individual to be left alone." Lawyer ***Brandeis*** is now Justice ***Brandeis*** of the Supreme Court. And the range of the individual's "right of privacy" is presented to the court for determination in the case of ***Olmstead v. United States.*** [60] It was a 5 to 4 decision. ***Brandeis*** was with the minority, joined by Holmes, Butler, and Stone. In one grandiloquent sweep ***Brandeis*** put a constitutional face on the right of privacy that was to exist as the legal seedbed for the proliferation of the right of privacy as we know it today.

Olmstead involved a federal criminal prosecution of ***Olmstead*** and others on the charge of conspiracy to violate the National Prohibition Act. Defendants were engaged in the massive importation of intoxicating liquors and in carrying out their operation extensive use was made of their private telephones. Evidence of the conspiracy resulted from the interception of telephone conversations of the defendants by federal prohibition officers. Telephone wires were inserted along the ordinary telephone wires from the residences and business office of the defendants. The insertion or tapping of the telephone wires was made without trespass upon any property belonging to the defendants. Transcripts were made of all the conversations recorded and such evidence was used to prove the guilt of the defendants. The defendants objected to the use of such evidence contending that the tapping of the telephone wires constituted an illegal search and seizure in violation of the Fourth Amendment and furthermore that the use of such recorded conversations compelled the defendants to be witnesses against themselves in violation of the Fifth Amendment and therefore their conviction must be reversed.

A majority of the five justices upheld the conviction of these defendants. In the process the majority asserted that the Fourth Amendment was to prevent the use of "governmental force to search a man's house, his person, his papers and his effects, and to prevent their seizure against his will." The court further observed that, "here we have testimony only of voluntary conversations secretly overheard." Further said the majority opinion:

> "There was no searching. There was no seizure. The evidence was secured by the use of the sense of hearing and that only. There was no entry of the houses or offices of the defendants."

The court also concluded that the Fifth Amendment was not violated because there was no evidence "of compulsion to induce the defendants to talk over their many telephones."

In his dissenting opinion, Justice Brendeis reminded that "the telephone is a public service furnished" by the authority of the federal government. He referred to an earlier decision of the court where it was held that opening a sealed letter constituted an illegal search. "There is, in essence," said Justice Brendeis, "no difference between the sealed letter and the private telephone message." Then he declared:

> "The evil incident to invasion of the privacy of the telephone is far greater than that involved in tampering with the mails. Whenever a telephone line is tapped, the privacy of the persons at both ends of the line is invaded, and all conversations between them upon any subject, and although proper, confidential, and privileged, may be overheard. Moreover, the tapping of the telephone of every other person whom he may call, or who may call him. As a means of espionage, writs of assistance and general warrants are but puny instruments of tyranny and oppression when compared with wire tapping."

Brandeis reminded that we live in a changing world. "Clauses guaranteeing to the individual protection against specific abuses of power," said ***Brandeis*** must have a "capacity of adaptation to a changing world." ***Brandeis*** referred approvingly to the ***Boyd*** decision earlier mentioned and then said:

> "But 'time works changes, brings into existence new conditions and purposes.' Subtler and more far-reaching means of invading privacy have become available to the government. Discovery and invention have made it possible for the government, by means far more effective than stretching upon the rack, to obtain disclosure in court of what is whispered in the closet."

Finally, apparently recalling his earlier days as a Boston lawyer in his crie de coeur to be "let alone," he postulated:

> "The makers of our Constitution undertook to secure con-

> ditions favorable to the pursuit of happiness. They recognized the significance of man's spiritual nature, of his feelings and of his intellect. They knew that only a part of the pain, pleasure and satisfactions of life are to be found in material things. They sought to protect Americans in their beliefs, their thoughts, their emotions and their sensations. They conferred, as against the government, the right to be let alone the most comprehensive of rights and the right most valued by civilized men. To protect that right, every unjustifiable intrusion by the government upon the privacy of the individual, whatever the means employed, must be deemed a violation of the Fourth Amendment. And the use, as evidence in a criminal proceeding, of facts ascertained by such intrusion must be deemed a violation of the Fifth."

Brandeis' notion of the right of privacy, as he stated it, was not vindicated until 1967, twenty-eight years after his tenure on the Supreme Court, when, in ***Katz v. United States*** [61], the Supreme Court ruled that unauthorized wiretaps violated the search and seizure clause of the Fourth Amendment.

Before going into a discussion of the next notable case, it is helpful to focus on the existing theory of liberty exemplifying the relationship of parents and their children. In the 1925 ***Pierce*** decision the court declared:

> "The fundamental theory of liberty upon which all governments of this union repose excludes any general power of the state to standardize its children by forcing them to

> accept instruction from public teachers only. *The child is not the mere creature of the state; those who nurture him and direct his destiny have the right, coupled with the* ***high duty,*** *to recognize and prepare him for additional obligations."*

This fundamental theory of the rights and duty of a parent to prepare his child for adulthood was so eroded away by later decisions as to deny a parent the right of consent before his minor daughter could have an abortion. Witness the unfolding judicial drama.

The 1965 case of ***Griswold v. State of Connecticut,***[62] signals the dramatic beginning of the radical expansion of the right of privacy of the individual. It engages a majority of the Supreme Court judges in substituting their subjective view of social policies for that of the legislative body of the State of Connecticut and in massaging the text of the several constitutional amendments to mold a constitutional meaning supportive of their social preferences; and, in the process, in bringing about a dramatic shift of power from the several states and the national congress to the Supreme Court, as the ultimate arbiter of the social and moral fabirc of our national character. The result of that decision, as to some, will live in infamy, and, as to others, will live in glory. The opinion of each judge is a study in the contrasting views of learned men regarding the constitutional framework of our system of government.

The ***Griswold*** case involved the constitutionality of a Connecticut law which prohibited the use of "any drug, medicinal article or instrument for the purpose of preventing conception" and provided a penalty of fifty dollars or imprisonment of not less than sixty days nor more that one year or both be imposed on any person "who assists, abets, counsels, causes, hires or commands another" to violate this law. ***Griswold***, Executive Director of the Planned Parenthood League of Connecticut, and Buxton, a licensed physician and a professor at the Yale Medical School who served as Medical Director for the League, were found guilty of violating this Connecticut law because they advocated and counseled the use of contraceptives as a means of preventing conception. The Supreme Court held that such a law was unconstitutional because it violated the constitutional right of privacy of individuals.

Significantly, the marital status of the defendants was not involved in this case. The essential involvement of these defendants was their conduct in advising married persons in the use of contraceptives. This gave the court the opportunity to latch on to the institution of marriage as the lynchpin of its decision. The court then rhapsodized about the institution of marriage in these words:

> "Marriage is a coming together for better or worse, hopefully enduring, and intimate to the degree of being sacred. It is an association that promotes a way of life, not causes; a harmony in living, not political faiths, a bilateral loyalty, not commercial or social projects. Yet it is an association for as noble a purpose as any involved in our prior decisions."

Suggesting alarm, the court then stated that the law in question prohibited "the <u>use</u> of contraceptives rather than regulating their manufacturer or sale," thus implying the nonexistent spectacle of the police invading the marital bedroom to investigate the use of contraceptives. The court then concluded that this law therefore "seeks to achieve its goal by means having a maximum destructive impact upon that relationship." The court then went in search of constitutional grounds to strike this state law with nullity. As a result of that search it concluded that the First, Third, Fourth, Fifth and Ninth Amendments of the Constitution were implicated. These were implicated because, the majority concluded, they involved the right of privacy. For example, the majority concluded that the Third Amendment which prohibits the quartering of soldiers "in any house in time of peace without the consent of the owner is another facet of that privacy." The Fourth Amendment also speaks to privacy because of its guarantees to the people of the "right of the people to be secure in their persons, houses, papers, and effects, against unreasonable searches and seizures." The Fifth Amendment was implicated because of the proscription against "self-incrimination" and thus "creates his own right of privacy which government may not force him to surrender to his detriment." The majority also concluded that the Ninth Amendment was involved because of its provision that "the enumeration of the Constitution of certain rights shall not be construed to deny or disparage others retained by the people." Unable to discover words used in these several Amendments that expressly speak to the right of privacy of the individual, the majority concluded that their "penumbras" gave rise to the right of privacy of the individual. This view of the majority was stated in these words:

> "The foregoing cases suggest that specific guarantees in the Bill of Rights have penumbras, formed by emanations from those guarantees that help give them life and substance."

In holding the state law unconstitutional, the majority asserted:

> "Such a law cannot stand in light of the familiar prin-

> ciple, so often applied by this Court, that a 'governmental purpose to control or prevent activities constitutionally subject to state regulation may not be achieved by means which sweep unnecessarily broadly and thereby invade the area of protected freedoms."

Before discussing the vigorous dissent in this case, a brief comment on the rationale of the majority opinion is indicated. As the majority opinion admits, it could discover nothing in the text of the several constitutional amendments mentioned that expressly spoke to the existence of the right of privacy interposed by the court to declare unconstitutional the Connecticut law in controversy. Instead, the majority relied on the "penumbras" of the several constitutional amendments as a basis for its decision. But then to understand this decision, one must ask, what is a penumbra? Webster defines a penumbra as follows:

> "The partly lighted area surrounding the complete shadow of a body, as the moon, in full eclipse; the less dark region surrounding the dark central area of a sunspot; vague, indefinite, or borderline area."

Such a definition sheds considerable light on the majority opinion. It tells us that the text of the several Amendments relied upon by the majority opinion is a dark area which sheds no light on the right of privacy interposed by the court in support of its opinion. The sole support for the opinion therefore is the "partly lighted area surrounding the complete shadow" of the text. Seemingly such a vague, indefinite, and borderline area of light, even if arguably workable, is scarcely a reliable tool to establish a consistent standard of judgment, much less to define the fundamental rights of our citizens. The hopeless flaw of such a constitutional interpretative approach is made manifest by the dissent.

THE DISSENT

Justice Hugo Black, joined by Justice Stewart, entered a vigorous dissent. His dissent is all the more significant, because Black has always been considered to be a liberal member of the court. However, he was not a liberal in the sense that he was given to taking flights on the wings of secularism, materialism and nihilism. He was a liberal who was always loyal to the text of the Constitution and applied a commn sense meaning to the words of the Constitution. For example, if the First Amendment provided that "congress shall make no law . . . abridging the freedom of speech" it meant just that as those words are commonly understood. His brand of liberalism is more classically characterized by his insistence that the Fourteenth Amendment incorporated all of the original amendments of the Constitution and these amendments, therefore, were applicable against all the states of the union for the benefit of all the people of the nation. It is in this context that his dissent in ***Griswold*** acquires its vitality and strength.

For starters, Black declared:

> "I do not to any extent whatever base my view that this Connecticut law is constitutional on a belief that the law is wise or that its policy is a good one...I feel constrained to add that the law is every bit as offensive to me as it is to my Brethren...There is no single one of the graphic and eloquent strictures and criticisms fired at the policy of this Connecticut law either by the court's opinion or by those of my concurring Brethren to which I cannot sub-

> scribe —<u>except their conclusion that the evil qualities they see in the law make it unconstitutional</u>."

Further Justice Black postulated that had the "doctor defendant here or either the non-doctor defendant" been convicted for doing nothing more than "expressing opinions to persons coming to the clinic that certain contraceptive devices, medicines or practices would do them good and would be desirable, or for telling people how devices could be used, I can think of no reason at this time why their expressions of views would not be protected by the First and Fourteenth Amendments, which guarantee freedom of speech." Black further stated:

> "But speech is one thing; conduct and physical activities are quite another."

Justice Black continued to observe that the defendants were active participants in an organization which gave physical examinations to women, advised them what kind of contraceptive devices or medicine would more likely be satisfactory for them and then "supply the devices themselves all for a graduated scale of fees, based on the family income." He concluded that they were engaged in "conduct" to help people violate the Connecticut law. The First and Fourteenth Amendment do not come into play simply because "some speech was used in carrying on the conduct." He lampooned the court's use of the right of privacy arising from the "penumbra" of the First Amendment thusly:

> "The Court talks about a constitutional 'right of privacy' as though there is some constitutional provision or provisions forbidding any law ever to be passed which might abridge the 'privacy' of individuals. **But there is not.**

> There are, of course, guarantees in certain specific constitutional provisions which are designed in part to protect privacy at certain times and places with respect to certain activities. Such, for example, is the Fourth Amendment's guarantee against 'unreasonable searches and seizures.'"

Justice Black then continued:

> "But I think it belittles that Amendment to talk about it as though it protects nothing but 'privacy.' To treat it that way is to give it a niggardly interpretation, not the kind of liberal reading I think any Bill of Rights provision should be given. The average man would very likely not have his feelings soothed any more by having his property seized openly than by having it seized privately and by stealth. He simply wants his property left alone. And a person can be just as much, if not more, irritated, annoyed and injured by an unceremonious public arrest by a policeman as he is by a seizure in the privacy of his office or home."

Further, Justice Black observed, to use words not found in the Constitution which are more or less flexible, gives license to distort the meaning of the Constitution and to supplant it with the social and political agenda of the one so interpreting the Constitution. This view is captured in his following eloquent statement:

> "One of the most effective ways of diluting or expanding a constitutionally guaranteed right is to substitute for the

> crucial word or words of a constitutional guarantee another or words, more or less flexible and more or less restricted in meaning, This fact is well illustrated by the use of the term 'right of privacy' as a comprehensive substitute for the Fourth Amendment's guarantee against 'unreasonable searches and seizures.' 'Privacy' is a broad, abstract and ambiguous concept which can easily be shrunken in meaning but which can also, on the other hand, easily be interpreted as a constitutional ban against many things other than searches and seizures. I have expressed the view many times that First Amendment freedoms, for example, have suffered from a **failure of the courts to stick to the simple language of the First Amendment in construing it,** instead of invoking multitudes of words **substituted for those the Framers used**."

In rejecting the Court's "right of privacy" rationale, Justice Black concluded:

> "For these reasons I get nowhere in this case by talk about a constitutional 'right of privacy' as an emanation from one or more constitutional provisions. I like my privacy as well as the next one, but I am nevertheless compelled to admit that **government has a right to invade it unless prohibited by some specific constitutional provision.** For these reasons I cannot agree with the Court's judgment and the reasons it gives for holding this Connecticut law unconstitutional."

Justice Black then addressed the due process and Ninth Amendment argument urged in support of striking down the Connecticut law. Justice Black asserted that an anlysis of that argument demonstrates that the argument as to both amendments turns out "to be the same thing, merely using different words to claim for this court and the federal judiciary power to invalidate any legislative act which the judge find irrational, unreasonable or offensive." Justice Black then stated:

> "This Court's belief that a particular state law under scrutiny has no 'rational or justifying' purpose, or is offensive to a 'sense of fairness and justice.' If these formulas based on 'natural justice,' or others which mean the same thing, are to prevail, they require judges to determine what is or is not constitutional on the basis of their own appraisal of what laws are unwise or unnecessary."

Implicating the separation of powers of our Constitutional system of government, Justice Black then emphasized:

> "The power to make such decisions is of course that of a legislative body. Surely it has to be admitted that no provision of the Constitution specifically gives such blanket power to courts to exercise such a supervisory veto over the wisdom and value of legislative policies and to hold unconstitutional those laws which they believe unwise or dangerous."

***

> "I do not believe that we are granted power by the Due

> Process Clause or any other constitutional provision or provision to measure constitutionality by our belief that legislation is arbitrary, capricious or unreasonable, or accomplishes no justifiable purpose, or is offensive to our own notions of 'civilized standards of conduct.' Such an appraisal of the wisdom of legislation is an attribute of the power to make laws, not of the power to interpret them. The use by federal courts of such a formula or doctrine or whatnot to veto federal or state laws simply takes away from Congress and States the power to make laws based on their own judgment of fairness and wisdom and transfers that power to this Court for ultimate determination — a power which was specifically denied to federal courts by the convention that framed the Constitution."

In rejecting the opinion of Justice Goldberg claiming that the Ninth Amendment, as well as the Due Process Clause rendered the Connecticut statute unconstitutional, Justice Black observed:

> "My Brother GOLDBERG has adopted the recent discovery that the Ninth Amendment as well as the Due Process Clause can be used by this Court as authority to strike down all state legislation which this Court thinks violates 'fundamental principles of liberty and justice,' or is contrary to the 'traditions and [collective] conscience of our people.' He also states, without proof satisfactory to me, that in making decisions on this basis judges will not consider 'their personal and private notions.' One may ask how they can avoid considering them. Our Court cer-

tainly has no machinery with which to take a Gallup Poll. And the scientific miracles of this age have not yet produced a gadget which the Court can use to determine what traditions are rooted in the '[collective] conscience of our people.'"

In speaking specifically to the Ninth Amendment Justice Black further elaborated:

"That Amendment was passed, not to broaden the powers of this Court or any other department of the 'General Government,' but, as every student of history knows, to assure the people that the Constitution in all its provisions intended to limit the Federal Government to the powers granted expressly or by necessary implication. If any broad, unlimited power to hold laws unconstitutional because they offend what this Court conceives to the '[collective] conscience of our people' is vested in this Court by the Ninth Amendment, the fourteenth Amendment, or any other provision of the Constitution, it was not given by the Framers, but rather has been bestowed on the court by the Court. This fact is perhaps responsible for the peculiar phenomenon that for a period of a century and a half no serious suggestion was ever made that the Ninth Amendment, enacted to protect state powers against federal invasion, could be used as a weapon of federal power to prevent state legislatures from passing laws they consider appropriate to govern local affairs. Use of any such broad, unbounded judicial authority would make of this

> Court's member a day-to-day constitutional convention."

Not wanting to be misunderstood in the slightest degree, Justice Black elaborated:

> "My point is that there is no provision of the Constitution which either expressly or impliedly vests power in this Court to sit as a supervisory agency over acts of duly constituted legislative bodies and set aside their laws because of the court's belief that the legislative policies adopted are unreasonable, unwise, arbitrary, capricious or irrational. The adoption of such a loose, flexible, uncontrolled standard for holding laws unconstitutional, if ever it is finally achieved, will amount to a great unconstitutional shift of power to the courts which I believe and am constrained to say will be bad for the courts and worse for the country. Subjecting federal and state laws to such an unrestrained and unrestrainable judicial control as to the wisdom of legislative enactments would, I fear, jeopardize the separation of governmental powers that the Framers set up and at the same time threaten to take away much of the power of States to govern themselves which the constitution plainly intended them to have."

Justice Black emphasized that he was not able to rely on any "mysterious and uncertain natural law concept as a reason for striking down this state law."

Justice Black then quoted from the earlier decision of the Supreme Court in ***Ferguson v. Skrupa*** [63]:

> "The doctrine that prevailed in Lochner, Coppage, Adkins, Burns, and like cases - that due process authorizes courts to hold laws unconstitutional when they believe the legislature has acted unwisely - has long since been discarded. We **have returned to the original constitutional proposition that courts do not substitute their social and economic beliefs for the judgment of legislative bodies, who are elected to pass laws."**

In speaking against the "personal preferences" of judges as a basis to interpret the Constitution, Justice Black adopted the words uttered by Judge Hand:

> "For myself it would be most irksome to be ruled by a bevy of Platonic Guardians, even if I knew how to choose them, which I assuredly do not."

POST MORTEM

Objective scrutiny of the majority opinion is necessary in order to understand the constitutional implication of that decision and the direction in which the court was taking our nation. As earlier stated the majoirty of the court insisted that constitutional Amendments 1, 3, 4, 5, and 9 were implicated and relied upon as a basis for the court's decision. These Amendments as they apply are set forth verbatim:

> Amendment 1:
>
> Congress shall make no law respecting an establishment of religion, or prohibiting the free exercise thereof; or abridging the freedom of speech, or of the press; or the right of the people peaceably to assemble, and to petition

the Government for a redress of grievances.

Amendment 3:
No Soldier shall, in time of peace be quartered in any house, without the consent of the Owner, nor in time of war, but in a manner to be prescribed by law.

Amendment 4:
The right of the people to be secure in their persons, houses, papers, and effects, against unreasonable searches and seizures, shall not be violated, and no Warrants shall issue, but upon probable cause, supported by Oath or affirmation, and particularly describing the place to be searched, and the persons or things to be seized.

Amendment 5:
No person shall be held to answer for a capital, or otherwise infamous crime, unless of a presentment or indictment of a Grand Jury, except in cases arising in the land or naval forces, or in the Militia, when in actual service in time of War or public danger; nor shall any person be subject for the same offence to be twice put in jeopardy of life or limb; nor shall be compelled in any criminal case to be a witness against himself, nor be deprived of life, liberty, or property, without due process of law; nor shall private property be taken for public use, without just compensation.

> Amendment 9:
> The enumeration in the Constitution, of certain rights, shall not be construed to deny or disparage others retained by the people.

The majority of the court acknowledged that none of the collective words of these Amendments spoke to the individual's right of privacy. Instead of engaging in deliberate analysis of the words of these Amendments and drawing reasonable inferences from them as a basis for the decision, the majority elected to avoid such an interpretation approach. Instead, the majority of the judges elected to rely upon the "penumbras" of these constitutional Amendments as a basis of the court's decision. Paradoxically, when reliance is placed upon the "penumbras" of the constitutional Amendments, that engages a judge in seeing what he wants to see in the bright light encircling the "shadow" of the textual body of the Amendments, "as the moon, in full eclipse." And the majority of the judges of the court saw in this circular bright light a right of privacy that rendered the Connecticut law unconstitutional, a law which prohibited the use of "any drug, mechanical article or instrument for the purpose of preventing conception" which the people of Connecticut felt was reasonably necessary to secure the welfare of Connecticut citizens. In addition to finding the light of truth surrounding the dark shadow of the textual body of these several Amendments, the majority of the court then substituted their words for the words of the several Amendments. Among the words selected by the majority of the justices are such terms as "right of privacy"; that a state law has no "rational or justifying purpose" or is offensive to a "sense of fairness and justice" or offensive to our notion of "civilized standards of conduct" or "fundamental principles of liberty and justice" or is contrary to the "traditions and conscience of our people," even though, as Justice Black points out, the Supreme Court has no machinery with which to take a Gallop Poll to determine what in the "conscience of the people" nor has there developed any scientific miracles, as Justice Black emphasizes, which the court can use to determine what traditions are "rooted in the [collective] conscience of our people." And the use by federal courts of such elastic terms and phrases to veto federal and state laws "simply takes away from Congress and the states the power to make laws based on their own judgment of fairness and wisdom and transfers that power " to the Supreme Court for "ultimate determination" - a power which was specifically denied to federal courts by the convention that framed the Constitution, as Justice Black points out.

Thus, the majority opinion exemplifies the building blocks, created by the majority of the judges, of radical liberalism, whereby a judge's social and political agenda is established and implemented, on the ruins of the original intent of the Framers of the Constitution, as the supreme law of the land. And because of our tripartite system of government, neither the executive not the legislative branches of government have the power to change the decision of the Supreme Court regarding constitutional issues, except throught the constitutional amendment process. The Supreme Court, however, may reverse itself on any issue, constitutional or statutory in nature. Thus there exists an alternative remedy to unacceptable decisions of the Supreme Court regarding the Constitution: nominating judges who will respect and uphold the separation of powers of our system of government and the original intent of the Framers of our Constitution. As Justice Black rationalizes "the use by federal courts of such a formula or doctrine or whatnot to veto federal or state laws simply takes away from Congress and States the power to make laws based on their own judgment of fairness and wisdom and transfers that power to this Court for ultimate determination — a power which was specifically denied to federal courts by the convention that framed that Constitution." Justice Black prophesied further alarming consequences resulting from the abuse of the power of judges as exemplified in this case. Said Justice Black:

> "The adoption of such a loose, flexible, uncontrolled standard for holding laws unconstitutional, if ever it is finally achieved, will amount to a great unconstitutional shift of power to the courts which I believe and am constrained to say will be bad for the courts and worse for the country. Subjecting federal and state laws to such an unrestrained and unrestrainable judicial control as to the wisdom of legislative enactments would, I fear, jeopardize the separation of governmental powers that the Framers set up and at the same time threaten to take away much of the power of States to govern themselves which the Constitution plainly intended them to have."

As subsequent decisions demonstrate Justice Black's prophecy, that the adoption of loose, flexible, uncontrolled standards for holding laws unconstitutional would result in "a great unconstitutional shift of power to the courts which I believe and am constrained to say will be bad for the courts and worse for the country" became a reality.

The 1965 judicial rationale of the ***Griswold*** decision gave birth to the constitutional right of abortion in the 1973 decision of the Supreme court in the case of ***Roe v. Wade.*** [64] Presented for decision in the ***Roe*** case was the constitutionality of a Texas statute, which made it a crime to procure an abortion or to attempt to do so, except with respect to "an abortion procured or attempted by medical advice for the purpose of saving the life of the mother." In her complaint to the federal district court, ***Roe*** alleged that she was "unmarried and pregnant"; that she wished to terminate her pregnancy by an abortion performed by a competent "licensed physician" but that she was uanble to obtain such an abortion in Texas, "because her life did not appear to be threatened by the continuation of her pregnancy." She further asserted that she could not afford to travel to another jurisdiction in order to secure a legal abortion where "her life did not appear to be threatened by the continuation of her pregnancy," and which was not required. She contended that the Texas statute abridged her right of personal privacy, protected by the 1st, 4th, 5th, 9th, and 14th Amendments.

At the outset of its opinion, the court admitted:

> "We forthwith acknowledge our awareness of the sensitive and emotional nature of the abortion controversy, of the vigorous opposing views, even among physicians, and of the deep and seemingly absolute convictions that the subject inspires."

Betraying a sense of judicial uncertainty and a daunting discomfort of apocrypha, the court went in search of ancient history to reassure itself of the legitimacy of what it was about to do. It was a search indigenous to a legislative body seeking to find support for its wisdom in enacting laws, rather than a search for legal precedents and legal principles indigenous to the action of a court in interpreting the constitutionality of a law enacted by a legislative body. Further, the court acknowledged that the subject of abortion was a complex one with many human factors contending for recognition. Said the court:

> "One's philosophy, one's experiences, one's exposure to the raw edges of human existence, one's religious training, one's attitudes toward life and family and their values, and the moral standards one establishes and seeks to observe, are all likely to influence and to color one's thinking and conclusions about abortion.
>
> In addition, population growth, pollution, poverty, and racial overtones tend to complicate and not to simplify the problem."

Unwittingly the court was implying that these were factors which the legislative bodies of the several states must have considered in the exercise of the legislative judgment in enacting abortion laws, including the one before the court for its decision. Nevertheless, in its search, the court discovered ancient attitudes about abortion. Said the court, "We are told that at the time of the Persian Empire abortifacients were known and that criminal abortions were severely punished." Contrariwise, the court said it was also told that "abortion was practiced in Greek times as well as in the Roman Era." But said the court, the "Ephesian, Soranos" often described as the greatest of ancient gynecologists, appear to have been generally opposed to Rome's prevailing free-abortion practices. The court then visited the Hippocratic Oath. Included in that oath was "I will not give to a woman a pessary to produce abortion." The court then spoke to the common law and concluded that an abortion from the 16th to the 18th week of pregnancy, the point of quickening, "was not an indictable offense." It concluded that after the point of quickening or "animation" abortion was prohibited as criminal. Prior to the point of quickening, however, the "fetus was to be regarded as part of the mother, and its destruction, therefore, was not homicide." The court then visited the English statutory law and reviewed the various parliamentary enactments of law on the subject of abortion. In reviewing the American law, the court concluded that the state of Connecticut was the first state to enact abortion legislation in 1821. It also discovered the position of the American Medical Association as early as 1859, when an AMA Committee "deplored abortion and its frequency" and characterized as "ignorance" a belief, "even among mothers themselves, that the fetus is not alive until after the period of quickening." In its resolution of 1871, the AMA concluded that it was "unlawful and unprofessional for any physician to induce abortion or premature labor without the concurrent opinion of at least one respectable consulting physician, and then always with a view to the safety of the child-if that be possible." In the process of this historical review, the court acknowledged that Christian doctrine, the same basic doctrine upon which America was founded, opposed abortion as sinful and morally wrong.

Ironically, the court drew no persuasive conclusion from its exhaustive review of ancient history as to the legitimacy of abortion or its morality, though it ostensibly was intended as a search for truth. At best, this review of ancient cultures exemplified but a collection of eclectic mores and legal practices rooted in insensitive human impulses and inadequate scientific knowledge. And apparently it was because of such deficiencies that the court implicitly did not place explicit reliance on such a history to decide the constitutionality of the Texas law at issue, except as it might have felt some comfort in authorizing the killing of a helpless human being in its mother's womb, because some public official, some two thousand plus years ago did that same thing. Instead the majority of the Supreme Court judges invoked and relied upon the individual's right of privacy, earlier found to exist in the bright circular light (penumbras) of the several amendments to the Constitution, as a basis to legitimate abortion. In the process of interposing the right of privacy of the individual as a basis for its opinion, the court expressly acknowledged that "the Constitution does not explicitly mention any right of privacy." The court then observed that "in a long line of decisions . . .the court has recognized that a right of personal privacy, or a guarantee of certain zones of privacy, does exist under the Constitution," as manifested under the First, Fourth, Fifth, and Ninth Amendments and "in the penumbras of the Bill of Rights." Further the court stated that "These decisions make in clear that only personal rights that can be deemed 'fundamental' or 'implicit in the concepts of ordered liberty,'"are included.

The court then concluded that:

> "This right of privacy is broad enough to encompass a woman's decision whether or not to terminate her pregnancy."

Thus, the court declared that this right of privacy is a "fundamental" constitutional right and as such it encompasses "a woman's decision whether or not to terminate her pregnancy." But said the court, "the pregnant woman cannot be isolated in her privacy." A state has an interest in intervening. But such an intervention is circumscribed by the showing of a "compelling state interest." Said the court:

> "Where certain 'fundamental rights' are involved, the Court has held that regulation limiting these rights may be justified only by a 'compelling state interest.'"

After demonstrating a "compelling state interest" any legislative enactment or state intervention, "must be narrowly drawn to express only the legitimate state interest at stake." Such a narrowing of interest excludes all broad limitations. Thus before a state could attempt to regulate a pregnant woman's fundamental constitutional right to an abortion it had to show that the state had a "compelling interest" to intervene and that the intervention had to be "narrowly drawn to express only the legitimate State interest at stake."

After thus characterizing and limiting the state's interest in regulating abortion it then decided the time period during which the state's "compelling interest" might be exercised. The court concluded that the time when the state could exercise its "important and legitimate interest in the health of the mother" begins "at approximately the end of the first trimester." The rationale for determining that "compelling" point of time is based on the conclusion that "until the end of the first trimester mortality in abortion may be less than mortality in normal childbirth." Then said the court:

> "It follows that, from and after this point, a State may regulate the abortion procedure to the extent that the regulation reasonably relates to the preservation and protection of maternal health."

Before this time, however, the State is without any power to interfere with the woman's right to abortion. In other words, before this time the state is without power to prevent the killing of a human being in the mother's womb. This rule of law was stated by the court in these words:

> "This means, on the other hand, that, for the period of pregnancy prior to this 'compelling' point, the attending

> physician, in consultation with his patient, is free to determine, without regulation by the State, that, in his medical judgment, the patient's pregnancy should be terminated. If that decision is reached, the judgment may be effectuated by an abortion <u>free of interference by the State.</u>"

During the course of its decision on this point the court acknowledged that Christian religion proclaimed the ensoulment of the human being occurred upon conception. The court opted instead to rely on comparable mortality data, as stated above, as a basis to authorize the killing of the human being in the womb of the mother, free of interference from the state, during the first trimester of pregnancy.

The court further spoke to not only the time when the State's compelling interest comes into existence, but to the extent of any regulation of abortion by a state. In so doing, the court ruled:

> "With respect to the State's important and legitimate interest in potential and legitimate interest in <u>potential life</u>, the 'compelling' point is at viability. This is so because the fetus then presumably has the capability of meaningful life outside the mother's womb. State regulation protective of fetal life after viability thus has both logical and biological justifications. If the state is interested in protecting fetal life after viability, it may go so far as to <u>proscribe</u> abortion during that period, except when it is necessary to preserve the life or health of the mother."

The court concluded that the state statute "sweeps too broadly" and therefore it was unconstitutional because this broad sweep interfered with the privacy right of a pregnant woman.

Thus the ***Roe v. Wade*** case postulated that a pregnant woman, in the exercise of her right of privacy, had the absolute right to an abortion during the first trimester of pregnancy. Neither the state nor the national government had any legal authority to interfere with such an abortion. The decision to destroy the human being in the mother's womb belonged to the mother and her physician and no one else.

Roe v. Wade was followed by substantial social unrest and fierce debate. Those who favored killing human being in the first trimester while in the mother's womb argued their position under the euphemistic banner of "pro-choice." Those opposing such killing argued their opposition under the banner of "pro-life." There were protest marches at the nation's capitol and even on the grounds of the Supreme Court. Talk shows presented the strident rhetoric of the "pro-choice" supporters and the alarming speech of the"pro-life" supporters. Frustration, secondary to a sense of helplessness to undo the decree of ***Roe v. Wade***, which authorized the killing of helpless human beings in their mothers' womb, gave rise to violence, including the bombing of abortion clinics and the consequent maiming and killing of those associated with such clinics. The ***Roe v. Wade*** decision became the seedbed for a multiplicity of court decisions, modifying and expanding the ***Roe v. Wade*** decree, creating a judicial emanation of confusion and autocracy, of convolution and political disconnection.

The circular light of the moon eclipse theory of constitutional law expounded in the ***Griswold*** case and effectively utilized by the court in ***Roe v. Wade,*** focused on another abortion case: the case of ***Planned Parenthood of Central Missouri v. Danforth of 1976.*** [65] The court anticipated this case as "a logical and anticipated corollary to ***Roe v. Wade,*** for it raises issues secondary to those that were then before the court. "Indeed, some of the questions now presented were forecasted and reserved in ***Roe***" said the court. In 1974, the legislature of Missouri enacted a law "for the control and regulation of abortions in Missouri during all stages of pregnancy." Three days after the act had became effective, the Planned Parenthood of cental Missouri, a not-for-profit Missouri Corporation which maintains a facility in Columbia, Missouri for the performance of abortion, and two physicians associated with this corporation filed a lawsuit to have this law declared unconstitutional. The several issues presented to the court for determination included the State's definition of viability, the informed consent of the woman to an abortion during the first twelve weeks of pregnancy, the spouse's consent to such an abortion, the parental consent for such an abortion by a minor child, the prohibited use of saline amniocentesis as a method or technique of abortion after the first twelve weeks of pregnancy, and record keeping requirements concerning such abortions and the standard of care of the physician performing the abortion.

DEFINITION OF VIABILITY. The Missouri state law defined viability as "that stage of fetal development when the life of the unborn child may be continued indefinitely outside the womb by natural or artificial life-supportive systems." Those attacking this state law contended that the definition "violates and conflicts with the discussion of viability" in ***Roe v. Wade***. The court held that this definition did not conflict with the definition in ***Roe***. While affirmatively stating that it was not the "proper function of the legislature or the courts to place viability" at a "specific point in the gestation period" primarily because viability may vary in point of time with each "pregnancy," generally the court held that "viability" is that stage of fetal development when the life of the unborn child may exist or the fetus is "potentially able to live outside the mother's womb" as declared in the ***Roe*** decision. The statutory definition was thus found to be acceptable.

WOMAN'S CONSENT. The Missouri statute required that prior to submitting to an abortion during the first twelve weeks of pregnancy, the woman must certify in writing her consent to the procedure and "that her consent is informed and freely given and is not the result of coercion." Those attacking the constitutionality of this state law argued that such a requirement violated the ***Roe v. Wade*** decree of the court. The court noted that the ***Roe*** decision established that the state "may not restrict the decision of the patient and her physician regarding abortion during the first state of pregnancy." The state law which insisted that "her consent is informed and freely given" did not restrict the decision of the patient and her physician regarding abortion during the first state of pregnancy. In support of the conclusion the court said:

> "The decision to abort, indeed, is an important, and often a stressful one, and it is desirable and imperative that it be made with full knowledge of its nature and consequences. The woman is the one primarily concerned, and her awareness of the decision and its significance may be assured, constitutionally, by the State to the extent of requiring her prior written consent."

SPOUSE'S CONSENT. The Missouri statute required the prior consent of the spouse of the woman "seeking an abortion during the first twelve weeks of pregnancy," unless "the abortions is certified by a licensed physician to be necessary in order to preserve the life of the mother." Missouri argued that this law was enacted in the light of Missouri's "perception of marriage as an institution"; that major change in "family status is a decision to be made jointly by the marriage partners"; that an abortion could possibly effect a woman's "child bearing potential" and as a consequence the state had a "compelling interest" in imposing a condition of spousal consent to an abortion fraught with such disruptive impact on the institution of marriage. The court held that Missouri could not constitutionally require the consent of the spouse as a condition for abortion during the first twelve weeks of pregnancy. In so ruling the court stated that it recognized "that the decision whether to undergo or to forego an abortion may have profound effects on the future of any marriage, effects that are both physical and mental, and possibly deleterious." Notwithstanding these factors the court said "we cannot hold that the state had the constitutional authority to give the spouse unilaterally the ability to prohibit the wife from terminating her pregnancy, when the state itself lacks that right" as the ***Roe v. Wade*** decision already determined. During the first stage of pregnancy, the court continued, only the physician and his patients make that decision. The state cannot delegate authority "to any particular person" to prevent abortion during the first stage of pregnancy when the state itself has no constitutional authority to prevent such an abortion. Since the woman is the one who physically bears the child, as between the husband and the wife, the balance "weighs in her favor" to the exclusion of the husband as to whether or not such an abortion shall take place. Finally the court held that this state law is "inconsistent with the standard enunciated in ***Roe v. Wade***" and is "unconstitutional."

PARENTAL CONSENT. The Missouri state law required that the consent of a parent must be obtained before an abortion could take place with respect to the first twelve weeks of pregnancy, "where the woman is unmarried and under the age of eighteen years," unless, "the abortion is certified by a licensed physician is necessary in order to preserve the life of the mother." In support of this law the State argued that certain decisions were considered by the state to be outside the scope of a minor's ability to act in her own best interest or in the interest of the public. Because of such minority the State has a "compelling interest" to subject minors "to more stringent limitations than are permissible with respect to adults." The state cited examples of laws "proscribing the sale of firearms and deadly weapons to minors without parental consent, the sale of cigarettes and alcohol beverages to minors and other similar regulations." The state pointed out testimony to the effect that children of tender years (even ages 10 and 11) have sought abortions. Finally the state argued that to permit a child to obtain an abortion without the counsel of an adult "who has responsibility or concern for the child would constitute an irresponsible abdication of the state's duty to protect the welfare of the minor."

The court acknowledge that it had long recognized that the state "has somewhat broader authority to regulate the activities of children than of adults." In matters of abortion, however, the court placed the minor child on the same constitutional level as an adult and held that to require parental consent was unconstitutional. In justifying that ruling the court said:

> "Just as with the requirement of consent from the spouse, so here, the State does not have the constitutional authority to give a third party an absolute, and possibly arbitrary, veto over the decision of the physician and his patient to terminate the patient's pregnancy, regardless of

the reason for withholding the consent."

The majority opinion further rationalized:

> "Constitutional rights do not mature and come into being magically only when one attains the state-defined age of majority. Minors, as well as adults, are protected by the Constitution and possess constitutional rights."

Thus the right of privacy, found to exist in the circular light of the moon eclipse theory of constitutional law in the ***Griswold*** case, eclipsed a parent's right of consent to abortion of his minor child. In so holding, the court concluded:

> "Any independent interest the parent may have in the termination of the minor daughter's pregnancy is no more weighty than the right of privacy of the competent minor mature enough to have become pregnant."

Stressing the decision in ***Roe*** and quoting from it, the court postulated that even with respect to the under-18-year-old pregnant minor, "the abortion decision and its effectuation must be left to the medical judgment of the pregnant woman's attending physician."

Such a rule of law gives rise to profound questions. There is no serious room for argument that a physician should have the last word, where pregnancy poses a thereat to the life of the pregnant woman. The decision making contemplated by ***Roe*** is exclusive of such a life-threatening condition. But in a non-threatening condition, what is there to decide by the physician? Only that the abortion can be safely performed. Which is the same as his exclusive decision regarding a life threatening condition. Everything being equal then, the woman's right to an abortion is an on demand right. It is ludicrous to believe the physician would counsel against the woman's request for an abortion to preserve and protect potential life. After all, he has a bias for abortion. He has a financial interest in performing the abortion. So ***Roe*** teaches that the woman's right of privacy entitles her to kill a human being in her womb. Before ***Roe*** the goal of all constitutional rights was to protect something of a personal interest, not to grant a right of lethal aggression against a helpless human being. One had the constitutional right to use all force reasonably necessary to protect his/her property and his/her body, including the resistence to unwanted sexual attack. But when a woman engages in sexual copulation and pregnancy results, the calculous of the right of privacy, authorizing the killing of the hapless and helpless victim of that of procreation, exists as but a humanly infertile concept of moral or legal behavior. It is a barbaric notion, without reasonable rationality, no less, and probably more, than is slavery.

The court made short shrift of the issues of whether or not saline amniocentesis should be banned as a technique for abortion, of the record keeping requirements, and of the further requirement that a physician must take such measures to encourage or sustain the life of the child, failing in which he would be liable to being prosecuted for the crime of manslaughter. As to the ban on the use of saline amniocentesis the court simply held that the state had overlooked certain beneficial data that rendered the law unreasonable, arbitrary, and, therefore, unconstitutional. As to the record keeping requirement, the court agreed that it was acceptable and could be constitutionally enforced. As to the standard of care imposed upon the physician performing the abortion, the court struck down that portion of the law based on its conclusion that the law did not distinguish between the period of viability and the subsequent stages of pregnancy; therefore, the law was unconstitutional to the extent that it indiscriminately applied to the time of viability, and thus violated the ***Roe v. Wade*** decision.

Thus in one fell swoop the institution of marriage and the cohesion of family, so frequently exalted by the court as the cellular core of a free society, were decimated, husbands and wives and their offsprings were treated as independent strangers to each other and sacrificed to the secular deity of judicial activism, to the usurpation of power otherwise institutionally structured to be shared with the other branches of government.

By 1992 it became apparent that even the Supreme Court was not immune to the contagion of divisiveness, vitriol and violence generated by the ***Roe v. Wade*** decision, as demonstrated by the court's decision of ***Planned Parenthood v. Casey***[66].

In this 1992 case the Supreme Court justices confronted the ***Roe*** decision again. The judges were extremely divided. Only three of the nine judges were able to agree on a common decision. Four of the nine judges were of the opinion that ***Roe v. Wade*** must be reversed as being without sound constitutional foundation. The intensity of the disagreement among these nine judges is best illustrated by the concurring opinion of Justice Blackmun, who wrote the ***Roe*** decision in 1973, nineteen years earlier. Justice Blacknum mounted a personal attack on Chief Justice Rehnquist, an act universally considered in the world of the judiciary as offensive to the protocol of judicial rectitude. For examples, Justice Blackmun stated that THE CHIEF JUSTICE had a "*stunted* conception of individual liberty"; and "in THE CHIEF JUSTICE's world a woman considering whether to terminate a pregnancy is entitled to no more protection than adulterers, murderers, and so called 'sexual deviates'"; "THE CHIEF JUSTICE's *cramped* notion of individual liberty"; "THE CHIEF JUSTICE's *narrow* conception of individual liberty." A reading of Justice Blackmun's concurring opinion makes it quite obvious that his attack on Chief Justice Rehnquist was apparently fueled by a consuming fear of having his ***Roe*** decision reversed. For example, after commenting that the court's approach in the ***Casey*** decision "is world's apart from that of THE CHIEF JUSTICE", yet, said Justice Blackmun, "in another sense, the distance between the two approaches is short-the distance is but a single vote." Justice Blackmun then interjected the following personal note:

> "I am 83 years old. I cannot remain on this Court forever, and when I do step down, the confirmation process for my successor well may focus on the issue before us today. That, I regret, may be exactly where the choices between the two worlds will be made."

At issue in the ***Casey*** case were provisions of the Pennsylvania Abortion Control Act: (1) The Act required that a woman seeking an abortion give her informed consent prior to the procedure and (1a) that she be provided with certain information at least twenty-four hours before the abortion is performed; (2) that informed consent of one parent be obtained for a minor prior to abortion but there was a proviso for a judicial bypass procedure, (3) that the woman seeking an abortion must sign a statement indicating that she has notified her husband except in a case of medical emergency and, (4) certain reporting requirements on the facilities providing abortion services were mandated. Before any of the provisions took effect, five abortions clinics and a physician representing himself and a class of doctors who provide abortion services brought a lawsuit seeking a declaratory judgment that each of the provisions was unconstitutional.

While the ***Casey*** court did not reverse ***Roe v. Wade*** (falling short by one vote) it did reverse some of the earlier cases dealing with the same issues presented, qualified the nature of the State's interest but maintained the central core of ***Roe v. Wade.*** The entire decision making process was a search for common grounds but ended up producing abysmal failure. The opening statement of the three judge joint statement heralds this failure:

> "Liberty finds no refuge in a jurisprudence of doubt. Yet 19 years after our holding that the Constitution protects a woman's right to terminate her pregnancy in its early stages, ***Roe v. Wade***, 410 U.S. 113, 93 S.Ct. 705, 35L.Ed.2d147 (1973), that definition of liberty is still questioned. Joining the respondents as *amicus curia*, United States, as it has done in five other cases in the last decade, again asks us to overrule ***Roe.***"

Furthermore, because of the division and violence generated by the ***Roe*** decision, the five judge majority of the court felt that the very legitimacy of the court as an institution was under siege and the three judges concurring on one common decision struggled valiantly to shore up the legitimacy of the court. But the four dissenting judges, including THE CHIEF JUSTICE, would have none of this, primarily because they reasoned that the court had overstepped its constitutional authority in the ***Roe v. Wade*** decision. But what follows is the essence of the majority opinion.

It will be recalled that, according to the ***Roe*** decision, the right of a state to regulate abortion was based upon the exercise of its "compelling interest" in the health of the mother and in protecting and promoting the essential life of the fetus. The majority of the judges in the ***Casey*** decision changed that standard of state intervention. The right of the state to regulate abortion was now based on and "undue burden standard", that is, whether the State's intervention unduly burdens a woman's ability to make a decision to have an abortion. Justice O'Conner, Kennedy and Souter, in their concurring opinion verbalized this new rule of law as follows:

> "Only where state regulation imposes an undue burden on a woman's ability to make this decision does the power of the State reach into the heart of the liberty protected by the Due Process Clause."

A more detailed statement of this change reads as follows:

> "To protect the cental right recognized by ***Roe v. Wade*** while at the same time accommodating the State's profound interest in potential life, we will employ the undue burden analysis as explained in this opinion. An undue burden exists, and therefore a provision of law is invalid, if its purpose or effect is to place a substantial obstacle in the path of a woman seeking an abortion before the fetus attains viability."

These three judges also rejected the rigid trimester framework of ***Roe***. This rejection was verbalized by these judges as follows:

> "We reject the rigid trimester framework of ***Roe v. Wade***.

> To promote the State's profound interest in potential life, throughout pregnancy the State may take measures to ensure that the woman's choice is informed, and measures designed to advance this interest will not be invalidated as long as their purpose is to persuade the woman to choose childbirth over abortion. These measures must not be an undue burden on the right."

The three judge joint decision held that it was constitutional to require a woman seeking an abortion to give her written consent after having viewed material required by the state law regarding abortion and giving that consent twenty-four hours before the abortion. Earlier cases to the contrary were overruled. The court, however, held that the requirement that the woman give notice to her husband prior to abortion was unconstitutional because it constituted an undue burden on the woman's right to an abortion and was therefore invalid, the court holding, "a husband has no enforcement right to require a wife to advise him before she exercises her personal choices."

The three judge court also held as constitutional the requirement of the consent of at least one parent for an unemancipated young woman under eighteen years to obtain an abortion. This decision, however, was based on the condition that if such a consent is not granted the minor may exercise the judicial bypass procedure by petitioning a court for permission to have the abortion. The inquiry of the court in such a circumstance is whether or not the minor child is found sufficiently mature to make an informed consent. The court also found constitutional the requirement that abortion facilities file a report on each abortion because such a procedure rationally furthers the state's legitimate interest in advancing the state medical knowledge concerning maternal health and prenatal life. It was also rationally related, the court held, to the state's legitimate interest in informing tax payers as to what is benefitting from public funds and what services the funds are supporting.

This decision not only accentuates the profound and pervasive disagreements among the Supreme Court justices over the ***Roe*** decision regarding a woman's right to have an abortion, it also demonstrates a substantial retreat from the constitutional overreach of ***Roe v. Wade***. In this dissent, Chief Justice Rehnquist captured this thought in these words:

> "The joint opinion, following its newly minted variation on *stare decisis,* retains the outer shell of *Roe v. Wade* . . ., but beats a wholesale retreat from the substance of that case."

While retreating from the constitutional overreach of the ***Roe*** decision, the majority increased the burden on the right of the state to regulate abortion by creating the "undue burden" obstacle for state intervention. The previous state burden of a "compelling interest" was a standardized legal concept offering easily recognizable guidelines to effectively assess the existence of a "compelling interest." On the other hand, however, the "undue burden" concept is a standardless one, relying for its recognition on the subjective view of a judge, allowing for the interplay of a judge's predilection and preferences in the decision making process, a veritable substitute of the rule of men for the rule of law. In short, this decision instances a desperate attempt by an ever dwindling majority to salvage the core decision of ***Roe*** and to shore up its continuance by making it more difficult for a state to interfere with that decision. But Chief Justice Rehnquist and Justices White, Scalia and Thomas waged an unrelenting attack on the majority decision. Chief Justice Rehnquist, speaking for himself and the three dissenting justices, stated:

> "We believe that ***Roe*** was wrongly decided, and that it can and should be overruled . . ."

THE CHIEF JUSTICE further commented that although the "trimester framework that formed the underpinning of ***Roe***" was rejected the three concurring justices adopted "a revised undue burden standard to analyze the challenged regulation." Said THE CHIEF JUSTICE:

> "We conclude, however, that such an outcome is an unjustified constitutional compromise, one which leaves the Court in a position to closely scrutinize all types of abortion regulations despite the fact that it lacks the power to do so under the Constitution."

In the course of his decision THE CHIEF JUSTICE pointed up the conflicting and contradictory decisions of the court since the ***Roe*** decision in his efforts to emphasize the unreliability of that decision. In commenting upon the "principle of justice so rooted in the traditions and conscience of our people as to be ranked as fundamental" adopted by the majority in ***Roe v. Wade,*** THE CHIEF JUSTICE emphasized that there is nothing in the "historical traditions" of the American people which support the view that the right to terminate one's pregnancy is "fundamental." On the contrary, THE CHIEF JUSTICE stated:

> "At the time of the adoption of the Fourteenth Amendment, statutory prohibitions or restrictions on abortion were commonplace; in 1868, at least 28 of the then-37

> States and 8 Territories had statutes banning or limiting abortion. J. Mohr, Abortion in America 200 (1978). By the turn of the century virtually every State had a law prohibiting or restricting abortion on its books."

THE CHIEF JUSTICE further observed:

> "By the middle of the present century, a liberalization trend had set in. But 21 of the restrictive abortion laws in effect in 1868 were still in effect in 1973 when *Roe* was decided, and an overwhelming majority of the States prohibited abortion unless necessary to preserve the life or health of the mother."

Based on the undisputed historical record Chief Justice Rehnquist concluded that there existed no support to classify the right to abortion as "fundamental" under the Due Process Clause of the Fourteenth Amendment.

Justice Scalia vigorously dissented. It was his view that ***Roe*** was without constitutional authority. Further Justice Scalia observed:

> "The emptiness of the 'reasoned judgment' that produced *Roe* is displayed in plain view by the fact that, after more than 19 years of effort by some of the brightest (and most determined) legal minds in the country, after more than 10 cases upholding abortion rights in this Court, and after dozens upon dozens of *amicus* briefs submitted in these and other cases, the best the Court can do to explain how it is that the word "liberty" *must* be thought to include the right to destroy human fetuses is to rattle off a collection

> of adjectives that simply decorate a value judgment and conceal a political choice."

Justice Scalia further criticized the new found concept of "undue burden." He asserted that the majority's effort to clarify that concept "makes clear only that the standard is inherently manipulable and will prove hopelessly unworkable in practice." Further said Justice Scalia:

> "The ultimately standardless nature of the 'undue burden' inquiry is a reflection of the underlying fact that the concept has no principled or coherent legal basis.
>
> * * *
>
> The 'undue burden' standard is not at all the generally applicable principle the joint opinion pretends it to be; rather, it is a unique concept created specially for these cases, to preserve some judicial foothold in this ill-gotten territory."

There is nothing in the Constitution, said Justice Scalia, creating a privacy right that includes the right to terminate pregnancy and thereby destroy a living human being. The ***Roe*** decision reflects a political choice rather than a decision founded in the Constitution. "It is not reasoned judgment that supports the court's decision; only personal predilection," said Justice Scalia. He then referred to Justice Curtis' warning contained in his dissenting opinion in the ***Dred Scott*** case as being "as timely today as it was 135 years ago:"

> "[W]hen a strict interpretation of the Constitution, accord-

> ing to the fixed rules which govern the interpretation of laws, is abandoned, and the theoretical opinions of individuals are allowed to control its meaning, we have no longer a Constitution; we are under the government of individual men, who for the time being have power to declare that the Constitution is, according to their own views of what it ought to mean."

Finally, Justice Scalia concluded:

> "The permissibility of abortion, and the limitations upon it, are to be resolved like most important questions in our democracy: by citizens trying to persuade one another and then voting."

The opinion of the court covers 93 printed pages.

The more the ***Roe*** decision is subjected to judicial scrutiny, the less convincing its constitutional underpinnings appear. It has generated extreme violence on the streets, extreme rhetoric on the political and religious pulpits and extreme division among the members of the Supreme Court. Thanks to ***Roe v. Wade***, we now have partial birth abortion. That type abortion engages the abortionist in extracting a human being, capable of living outside the womb, from the mother's womb until its head protrudes outside sufficiently to allow the abortionist to kill it by penetrating the skull and sucking out its brain. If this human being were totally extracted from his mother's womb, the killing of it would be an act of murder. Abortion as we know it has been characterized by Pope John Paul II as springing from a culture of death. [67] On June 12, 1999, while at Zamosc, Poland, Pope John Paul II characterized the tragic irony of abortion and illegal tampering with human life in these words:

> "Is it really possible to oppose the destruction of the environment while allowing, in the name of comfort and convenience, the slaughter of the unborn and the procured death of the elderly and the infirm, and the carrying out, in the name of progress, of unacceptable interventions and forms of experimentation at the very beginning of human life?"

But shining through the ***Casey*** decision is a bright ray of hope for a return to constitutional sanity. What separates the killing from the right of the helpless human being to life is one vote in the Supreme Court. Hopefully that may soon come to pass. Until this comes about, the killing goes on.

EPILOGUE

Cosmologists, physicists, and astrophysicists have been peering into the universe, reaching lightyears into the past [68], in an effort to discover evidence as to the origin of the universe and man's relationship to such universe. Believing that the substance and light swirling about us are the creation of something, the search goes on. It has been theorized that at some time in the past, many lightyears ago, all material of the universe was compressed to the point of infinity in one location, generating incomprehensible heat, which triggered a cosmic explosion propelling all material of the universe into the void of the universe. This theory is called the "big bang" theory of creation. In support of that theory the scientific community has watched and confirmed particles of the material constantly hurtling through space on an endless journey. That conclusion or theory is based upon what scientists believe occurred one millisecond after the big bang. But before one millisecond there is a barrier to understanding the prior state of the universe. Thus far no one has been able convincingly to verify the existence of any force or condition regarding the prior state of the universe.

Recently scientists have discovered a "baby galaxy" that may have existed since the dawn hours of creation, maybe some thirteen billion years ago. So far as can be determined the space between earth and this baby galaxy is "flat" or geometrically normal. Such flatness in our cosmos may explain a genesis that was hospitable to life on earth. Scientists also have speculated that there exists a mother universe and "this first universe created itself and was its own mother, making the first matter in some way we will never be able to know", said J. Richard Scott. To me that sounds like our concept of a "God." And that reaction has occurred to some of the scientists. In fact Allan Sandage, one of the scientific explorers, has told a gathering that contemplating the majesty of the big bang helped to make him a believer in God, willing to accept that creation could only be explained as a "miracle." And such evidence has brought about a warming of the relationship between the scientific and spiritual disciplines. The effect of that warming induced some scientists to meet in Berkley, California in 1998, to discuss the startling findings of the scientific community that implicate the spiritual view of creation, as exemplified by the genesis of creation contained in the Old Testament.

We were reminded by the court in the notorious Dred Scott case that the founders of our nation were "high in literary accomplishments" and "high in their sense of honor, and incapable of asserting principles inconsistent with those on which they were acting." We, therefore, know that they were knowledgeable of human history, ancient and contemporary. They were aware of the genesis of creation as proclaimed by the Old Testament. They were also aware of its proclamations, that God spoke to the ancient prophets regarding matters ontological, imparting to them laws for the behavior of man and that there would appear on earth a Messiah, an expected savior or liberator of the people, especially the Jews. Their senses told them that there is a quality resonating in each of us which generates an ineffable yearning for something beyond the visible created world, a mystical something which has been worshiped by man in various forms throughout recorded history.

They were also familiar with the New Testament, which recorded the arrival of the expected Messiah in the person of Jesus Christ, His death on the cross and His resurrection. They learned of the pharisee Paul, who persecuted the early Christians; of his extraordinary experience at Damascus, when he was infused with the word of the Holy Spirit and became the martyred apostle of Christ; and who by his writings articulated the soteriological nature of the Christian religion, that is, a religion of salvation, a religion which proclaims that there is life after death. And the righteous will experience the ultimate truth, which is, coming face to face with God never before seen. It is a religion based on faith, hope and love, the latter being the pervasive ultimate of all three. Strengthened by this faith the founders of our nation were able to walk through the atheistic/rationalistic writings of their contemporaries, including Diderot, Grimm and Voltaire, and, buoyed by the thunderous voice of hope of Jean Jacques Rosseau, they fashioned a proclamation of government whose infrastructure was that of Christian morality. And this proclamation is captured in the Declaration of Independence:

> "We hold these truths to be self-evident; that all men are created equal; that they are endowed by their Creator with certain unalienable rights; that among these are life, liberty and the pursuit of happiness. That, to secure these rights, governments are instituted among men, deriving their just power from the consent of the governed . . ."

Early on, and no later than 1869, the Supreme Court recognized the Creator's involvement in the creation of America. Justice Field in the ***Slaughterhouse case*** validated that creative aphorism by declaring that unalienable rights mentioned in the Declaration of Independence were "rights which are the gift of the Creator; which the law does not confer but only recognizes." Thus these unalienable rights constitute an integral part of America's fundamental rights, and are, therefore, inseparable from our basic philosophy of government. In unabashly recognizing these rights, the court felt no impairment of duty or function, arising from conscience or from the separation of church and state. It perceived no constitutional wall of separation that interfered with or interdicted the court from paying tribute to God or acknowledging his involvement in the creation and existence of America. On the contrary, we as a nation have proclaimed to the world our faith in God by imprinting on our coin, "In God We Trust" and by daily invoking his superintendence in the opening of the House and Senate and other public institutions and in the taking of an oath of office.

Thus by the very nature of our philosophy of government there cannot exist a wall of separation between religious belief, or religion and the secular interests of government. At most, philosophically speaking, there is an element of prudent tolerance in the interfacing of these diverse interests - - a tolerance which accommodates the prudent existence of each, while creating a balance which inhibits the extreme function of either. For example, it would be an oxymoron to assert that included in the compass of unalienable rights would be the rights of degeneracy, obscenity, and human degradation, simply because the God whose existence we recognize would never include degeneracy, obscenity and human degradation as gifts to us from Him. To perpetuate these unalienable rights and the philosophic nature of our nation, our departments of government, including the judiciary, must exercise that measure of wisdom in creating and implementing our laws, that will give effect to that balance which will insure the effective co-existence of the religious and secular interests of our nation. To do otherwise is to invite religious bigotry with its concomitant oppression, or secular anarchism with its concomitant hedonistic degradation. During the last five decades we have traveled perilously down the road in the direction of the latter alternative. And how did this come about?

As stated earlier any usurpation of power by anyone of the three branches of government results in a meltdown of the structural integrity of government and a consequential dysfunction of the political process. Usurpation of power by the judicial department of government, especially in the area of individual constitutional liberty, is more devastating than such abuse by the other two branches. Firstly, the judiciary is the ultimate arbiter of the actions of the two other branches. Secondly, as to constitutional issues, the two other branches are without remedy against the constitutional decisions of the court, except the exercise of their power to initiate Amendments to the Constitution, a long and tedious process, whose success is always precarious, and, even if successful, the result could yet again be the victim of judicial abuse. It appears that what America is today, internally speaking, namely, a distortion of our traditional values, a disruption of family values and unity, pitting minors against parents and wives against husbands, an erosion of community bonds, and a disconnection of citizens from government, is due in large measure to the action of the judges at the highest level of government in substituting their social agendas for the law, by eschewing guiding principles of judicial interpretation, especially in matters involving the constitutional liberty of the individual *vis-a-vis* the majority will of the people.

In order to achieve and experience the ideals of our system of self-government our founders intended that the liberty of the individual is one of ordered liberty. As the court said in the 1937 ***Parrish*** case, "liberty in a **social organization**" is that which "requires the protection of law against the evils which menace the health, safety, moral and welfare of the people." In order to secure the "welfare of the people", the rule of law provides that the citizen must endure "all kinds of restraints and burdens." This means, the court further observed, that "there is no absolute freedom to do as one wills."

Not only is there a limitation imposed on the liberty rights of the individual, in furtherance of the ordered liberty of society, there is a principled limitation imposed on judges. For example, judges are to decide constitutional issues "with the best light we can obtain on the subject and to administer it as we find it, according to its true intent and meaning [of the Constitution] when it was adopted," so declared the ***Dred Scott*** case. And as ***Holmes*** said in the 1903 ***Otis and Gassman*** case, "While the courts must exercise a judgment of their own, it by no means is true that every law is void which may seem to the judges who pass upon it excessive, unsuited to its ostensible end, or based upon conceptions of morality with which they disagree." Under this principled interpretation process the state has the ultimate authority to eliminate what it believes to be an "admitted evil" even by prohibiting a calling or transaction "not in itself necessarily objectionable" and when a state exercises that authority "the courts cannot interfere unless, in looking at the substance of the matter, they can see that it 'is a clear, unmistakable infringement of rights secured by the fundamental law.'" Otherwise, said Holmes, "a constitution, instead of embodying only relatively fundamental rules of right, as generally understood by all English-speaking communities, would become the partisan of a particular set of ethical or economical opinions, which by no means are held *semper ubique et ab omnibus*." (always, everywhere, and from everyone) When the court, in the exercise of excessive power, and in violation of this paradigm of constitutional interpretation, denies to the people the fruits created by the legislatures of their state, the court thus "turns, as it were, what was meant for bread into a stone," as stated by Justice Swayne in the ***Slaughterhouse*** case. Tragically for the last several decades the people of America have been on a steady diet of stones.

This stone diet is best reflected in the area of free speech. The meaning of and the right to protect free speech were tested in the 1957 ***Roth*** case. In that case the court assured America that free speech and press were fashioned "to assure unfettered interchange of ideas for the bringing about of political and social changes desired by the people." And in that context the court proclaimed that "all ideas having even the slightest redeeming social importance - - unorthodox ideas, controversial ideas, even ideas hateful to the prevailing climate of opinion" were protected. But, emphasized the court, "implicit in the history of the First Amendment is the **rejection** of obscenity as utterly without redeeming social importance." Significantly, the court further postulated that what is obscene speech must be left to the determination of "the average person, applying contemporary community standards." In so ruling the court upheld the right of the people of California to enact laws to protect the moral fiber of society against obscene speech. But by 1969 obscene material containing obscene speech was declared by the Supreme Court as protected by the First Amendment right of free speech. The rapidity of this growth was aided by the court's discovery of new species of speech. In the 1971 ***Cohen*** case the court discovered emotive speech, a species of "inexpressible emotions." There the court was dealing with the words "Fuck the draft." The court held that such speech was protected by the First Amendment. Who, in his wildest imagination, could believe that the founders of our nation, who believed in the existence of a Supreme Being, ever contemplated that the First Amendment would protect such vulgarity and ribaldry as a concomitant part of public speech? This decision is a classic example of the court tolerating public speech more by respecting it less. Thus what was vulgar and lewd in 1942 was in 1971 "another's lyric." The court additionally discovered symbolic speech under the auspices of which all forms of naked obscene body movements are considered speech protected by the First Amendment. A picture of the crucifix in urine is now considered protected speech.

Tagging along with these newly discovered species of speech was the expansion of the right of privacy. This right of privacy reached its ultimate stretch when the court declared that it conferred on females the right to kill a defenseless human being in the mother's womb. And such a right of privacy exists even though the majority of the judges of the Supreme Court is unable to decipher its existence in the text of the Amendments to the Constitution. The majority discovered its existence in the penumbras of the several constitutional amendments, that is, the bright light encircling the "shadow" of the textual body of the amendments, "as the moon, in full eclipse." To reach the existence of this contorted meaning of the Constitution the majority judges substituted their words for the words of the several amendments. Such words as "right of privacy," "rational or justifying purpose" or "sense of fairness and justice" or "civilized standards of conduct" etc. Thus the majority opinion exemplifies the building blocks, created by the majority of the judges, of radical liberalism, whereby a judge's social and political agenda is esatblished and implemented, on the ruins of the original intent of the framers of the Constitution, as the supreme law of the land. Such judicial abuse is fraught with extreme danger to the American ideals of government. The nature of that danger is eloquently stated by Justice Black in the 1965 ***Griswold*** case. Said Justice Black:

> "The adoption of such a loose, flexible, uncontrolled standard for holding laws unconstitutional, if ever it is finally achieved, will amount to a great unconstitutional shift of

> power to the courts which I believe and am constrained to say will be bad for the courts and worse for the country. Subjecting federal and state laws to such an unrestrained and unrestrainable judicial control as to the wisdom of legislative enactments would, I fear, jeopardize the separation of governmental powers that the Framers set up and at the same time threaten to take away much of the power of States to govern themselves which the Constitution plainly intended them to have."

Justice Black's prophecy materialized in the ***Roe v. Wade*** decision, where on demand a pregnant female, including minors, have the constitutional right to destroy a human being in the mother's womb, without the consent of the husband or of the father of the minor. This constitutional right is founded on what the court has declared to be the right of privacy. As earlier mentioned, the majority of the judges of the Supreme Court were unable to discover in the text of the several constitutional amendments the existence of a right of privacy. But the majority found the existence of the right of privacy not in the text of the Constitution but in the penumbras, that is, the circular light around the darkness of the constitutional amendments, as a moon in full eclipse. And based on such a nebulous foundation more that one million human beings are slaughtered annually in the mother's womb. In the last major decision regarding abortion which occurred in 1992, five of the Justices voted to maintain in existence the central core of ***Roe v. Wade*** while four of the Justices dissented and unanimously declared that there existed no constitutional basis for the right of privacy reflected in the ***Roe*** decision and that the ***Roe*** decision itself is unconstitutional. As Justice Scalia said, "it is not reasoned judgment that supports the court's decision; only personal predilection." In emphasizing the great danger to America that such an unreasoned decision poses, Justice Scalia quoted the opinion of Justice Curtis, uttered more than one hundred and thirty-five years ago, declaring it "as timely today as it was one hundred and thirty-five years ago"' when Justice Curtis said:

> "[W]hen a strict interpretation of the Constitution, according to the fixed rules which govern the interpretation of laws, is abandoned, and the theoretical opinions of individuals are allowed to control its meaning, we have no longer a Constitution; we are under a government of individual men, who for the time being have power to declare that the constitution is, according to their own views of what it ought to mean."

Such judicial usurpation, when carried to an extreme, as is the case at this time, becomes a matter of judicial despotism. The fear of such despotism was verbalized by Justice Nathan Clifford in 1874, in the case of ***Loan Association v. Topeka*** [69], in these words:

> "Courts cannot nullify an act of the state legislature on the vague ground that they think it opposed to a general latent spirit supposed to pervade or underlie the Constitution, where neither the terms nor the implications of the instrument disclose any such restriction. Such a power is denied to the courts, because to concede it would be to make the courts sovereign over both the Constitution and the people, and convert the government into a judicial despotism."

The power of our nation originates with the people. The moral fiber of our democracy, therefore, is only as vibrant as the civic virtues of its people. If honesty, integrity and morality are to be returned to public life, the energy to fuel the machinery of change must originate with the caring people of America. We must return to the people the ideals upon which America was founded. We must make public officials responsive to the will and desires of the people and we must demand that judges of the highest court in the land be loyal to the founding structure and principles of America, to the end that our founding beliefs and ideals will be honored and respected by officials at the highest level of government. As Pope John Paul II recently observed:

> "There is no meaning in democracy or human rights if there is no meaning in anything. And there is no meaning in anything unless there is an Author of human rights and moral truth."

FOOTNOTES

1. Will Durant: The Life of Greece

2. In his effort to convert the Gentiles, St. Paul (Saul) utilized some of the Greek paganistic rituals and some of their ancient theology from time to time to proclaim the virgin birth, death, and resurrection. See Will Durant: Ceasar and Christ.

3. Patrick J. Buchanan: The Great Betrayal. This is an excellent statement on the virtue of tariffs and the vice of free trade.

4. James Truslow Adams: The March of Democracy.

5. Marbury v. Madison, 5 U.S. 137. While the court concluded that Madison was subject to the issuance of a writ of mandamus, it declined to issue it, after concluding that its original jurisdiction did not include mandamus.

6. Barron v. Baltimore. 32 U.S. (7 Pet.) 243 (1833).

7. Alexis de Tocqueville: Democracy in America.

8. Scott v. Sandford, 60 U.S. (19 How.), 393 (1857).

9. Slaughterhouse Case, 83 U.S. 36, (1873).

10. James Truslow Adams: The March of Democracy.

11. Allgeyer v. State of Louisiana, 165 U.S. 578, 17 S.Ct. 427 (1897).

12. Lochner v. New York, 198 U.S. 45, 25 S.Ct. 539 (1905).

13. James Truslow Adams: The March of Democracy.

14. Adair v. United States, 208 U.S. 161, 28 S.Ct. 277 (1908).

15. James Truslow Adams: The March of Democracy.

16. Coppage v. State of Kansas, 236 U.S. 1, 35 S.Ct. 240 (1915).

17. Atkins v. Children's Hospital, 261 U.S. 525, 43 S.Ct. 394 (1923).

18. West Coast Hotel Company v. Parrish, 300 U.S. 379, 57 S.Ct. 578 (1937).

19. Minna Irving: Betsy's Battle Flag.

20. Julia Ward Howe: The Flag.

21. Lucy Larcom: The Flag.

22. Minersville School District, et al v. Gobitis, et al., 310 U.S. 586, 60 S.Ct. 1010 (1940).

23. West Virginia State Board of Education, et al. v. Barnette, et al, 319 U.S. 624, 63 S.Ct. 1178 (1943).

24. James Truslow Adams: The March of Democracy.

25. Texas v. Johnson, 491 U.S. 397, 109 S.Ct. 2533 (1989).

26. Chaplinsky v. State of New Hampshire, 315 U.S. 568, 62 S.Ct. 766 (1942).

27. John Greenleaf Whittier: Barbara Frietchie.

28. Oliver Wendell Holmes: Old Ironsides.

29. Abraham Coles: The Microcosm and Other Poems

30. Henry Holcomb Bennett: The Flag Goes By.

31. Truax v. Corrigan, 257 U.S. 312, 42 S.Ct. 124 (1921).

32. Gitlow v. People of the State of New York, 268 U.S. 652, 45 S.Ct. 625 (1923).

33. Abrams, et al v. United States, 250 U.S. 616, 40 S.Ct. 17 (1919).

34. United States v. Carolene Products Co., 304 U.S. 144, 58 S.Ct. 778 (1938).

35. Palko v. State of Connecticut, 302 U.S. 319, 58 S.Ct. 149 (1939).

36. Otis v. Gassman v. Parker, 187 U.S. 606 (1903), 23 S.Ct. 168 (1903).

37. Reynolds v. United States, 98 U.S. 245 (1878).

38. Cantwell, et al v. State of Connecticut, 310 U.S. 296, 60 S.Ct. 900 (1940).

39. Everson v. Board of Education of Ewing, Tp., et. al, 330 U.S. 1, 67 S.Ct. 504 (1947).

40. People of State of Illinois v. Board of Education, 333 U.S. 203, 68 S.Ct. 461 (1948).

41. Braunfeld v. Brown, 336 U.S. 599, 81 S.Ct. 1144 (1961).

42. Sherbert V. Verner, 374 U.S. 398, 83 S.Ct. 1790 (1963).

43. Epperson v. Arkansas, 393 U.S. 97, 89 S.Ct. 266 (1968).

44. Lynch v. Donnelly, 465 U.S. 668, 104 S.Ct. 1355 (1984).

45. Chaplinsky v. New Hampshire, 315 U.S. 568, 62 S.Ct. 766 (1942).

46. The American Century: by Harold Evans.

47. Beauharnais v. People of the State of Illinois, 343 U.S. 250, 72 S.Ct. 725 (1952).

48. Roth v. United States, 354 U.S. 476, 77 S.Ct. 1304 (1957).

49. New York Times v. Sullivan, 84 S.Ct. 710 (1964).

50. Valentine v. Chrestenson, 62 S.Ct. 920 (1942).

51. Stanley v. Georgia, 89 S.Ct. 1243 (1969).

52. Cohen v. California, 403 U.S. 15, 91 S.Ct. (1780).

53. Clark v. Community for Creative Non-Violence, 104 S.Ct. 3065 (1984).

54. Barnes v. Glen Theatre, Inc., 111 S.Ct. 2456 (1991).

55. National Endownment for the Arts. v. Finley, 118 S.Ct. 2168 (1998).

56. Boyd v. United States, 116 U.S. 616, 6 S.Ct. 524 (1886).

57. Allgeyer v. State of Louisiana, 165 U.S. 161, 28 S.Ct. 277 (1897).

58. Meyer v. State of Nebraska, 42 S.Ct. 625 (1923).

59. Pierce v. Society of the Sisters of the Holy Names, et al, 48 S.Ct. 571 (1925).

60. Olmstead v. United States, 48 S.Ct. 564 (1928).

61. Katz v. United States, 48 S.Ct. 564 (1928).

62. Griswold v. State of Connecticut, 85 S.Ct. 1678 (1965).

63. Ferguson v. Skrupa, 83 S.Ct. 1028 (1963).

64. Roe v. Wade, 73 S.Ct. 765 (1973).

65. Planned Parenthood of Central Missouri v. Danforth of 19976, 96 S.Ct. 2831.

66. Planned Parenthood of Southeastern Pennsylvania v. Casey, 112 S.Ct. 2791 (1992).

67. Crossing the Threshold of Hope, by Pope John Paul, II.

68. Lighyear: A unit of length interstellar astronomy equal to the distance that light travels in one year in a vacuum or about 5,878,000,000,000 miles.

69. Loan Association v. Topeka, 87 U.S. 655.